MIDNIGHT BABY

MIDNIGHT BABY

AN AUTOBIOGRAPHY

DORY PREVIN

MACMILLAN PUBLISHING CO., INC.

NEW YORK

Printed in the United States of America

ACKNOWLEDGMENTS: "My Daddy Says I Ain't His Child,"
"The Veterans' Big Parade," and "Esther's First Communion" ©
Copyright 1970 Mediarts Music, Inc. and Bouquet Music. All rights
administered by United Artists Music Co., Inc. Used by permission.
"After Shock" and "Scared to Be Alone" © Copyright 1971 Mediarts
Music, Inc. and Bouquet Music. All rights administered by United
Artists Music Co., Inc. Used by permission. "Alice Blue Gown"
(Words: Joseph McCarthy; Music: Harry Tierney) Copyright ©
1919, renewed 1946, Leo Feist, Inc. Used by permission. "My Blue
Heaven" (Words: George Whiting; Music: Walter Donaldson)
Copyright © 1925, 1927, renewed 1952, 1954, Leo Feist, Inc. Used
by permission. "I'm Shooting High" (Words: Ted Koehler; Music:
Jimmy McHugh) Copyright © 1935, renewed 1962, Robbins
Music Corporation. Used by permission. "The Final Flight of the
Hindenburg" (Words and Music by Dory Previn) Copyright © 1971
Mediarts Music, Inc. and Bouquet Music. All rights administered by
United Artists Music Co., Inc. Used by permission. "Left Hand
Lost" (Words and Music by Dory Previn) Copyright © 1972 United
Artists Music Co., Inc. and Bouquet Music and Mediarts Music, Inc.
All rights administered by United Artists Music Co., Inc. Used by
permission. "My Daddy Says I Ain't His Child," "After Shock,"
"The Veterans' Big Parade," "Esther's First Communion," "Scared
to Be Alone," and "The Final Flight of the Hindenburg" from Dory
Previn's On My Way to Where, reprinted by permission of Bantam
Books, Inc. "The Lady in Red" Copyright © 1935 Warner Bros. Inc.
Copyright renewed. All rights reserved. Used by permission.

For Mike and Flo—we even had some fun.

Sometimes at night I light
a lamp so as not to see.

—ANTONIO PORCHIA

. . . in that narrow diary of my mind.

—ANNE SEXTON

I'll run away till I am bigger,
but then I'll fight.

—SHAKESPEARE

PREFACE

I don't think I wrote this book. I think I wrote it down.
For someone else. Someone I used to be. About three
years ago I began to see a little girl. Every time I closed
my eyes, she was there. Standing under a faintly familiar
tree. Looking at me. Waiting for something. I told this to
my therapist. He warned me to stop the spiritual shit, as
he called it. He was right, I suppose. I had a history of
seeing and hearing things. Usually, something of this sort
was a sign I was getting back into dangerous areas. But I
recognized this child. I knew her story. I also knew I
couldn't write any kind of book about my life today until
I let her tell about her life yesterday. And her life took me
into places I wanted to forget. But I couldn't forget. I
couldn't get away from her. She had to be dealt with. I
quit therapy and spent four, maybe five, weeks alone. In
the dubious security of my own house, I gave up. I ac-
knowledged her image. I broke with so-called reality. I
seemed divided into two people. A woman and a child.
The woman was dumb enough to think she was in charge.
The two argued, bickered, made up, rationalized, and
fantasized. The child grew stronger. Finally, the woman
gave in. All right, I shouted, I'll say it for you! When? Tomorrow. How about right now? No! *I want my say!* All
right, dammit, now! I sat down and started to write in the
words of the little girl. Later I tried to polish it a bit.

Adults haven't the sense to let well enough alone. But the original form belongs to the child. As she demanded it be told. In her voice. This book is her say.

Los Angeles   DORY PREVIN
April 1976

MIDNIGHT BABY

1

Screaming. Somebody was screaming in the plane. I felt
bad for whoever it was. But I felt good for myself. It had
been a great ride to the airport. The Los Angeles sky was
cloudless. My ticket was stamped. My luggage checked.
No anxieties. I was free of panic. It was over for me at
last. I was sure I had beaten it. Finally. And when I got to
the waiting room I had become absolutely certain. I had
looked out the window of the terminal and the plane had
smiled at me. I smiled back at the plane. We knew. Every
plane in the world had begged for this mission. And the
one with the finest credentials was picked. The best. The
bravest. The proudest. No wonder it was smiling. This
time I'd get to London. The plane was indestructible. I
was invincible. The center of the universe. As good as
presidents and kings. Mighty Lak a Rose. Shooting High!

2

The seat next to mine was empty. Sidney Poitier was late.
But that was okay. Mrs. Previn? Yes. Welcome aboard.
Thank you. Anything we can do, just ask. Thank you very
much. The door closed. Wait a minute. The sign went on.
The motors revved up. The plane shook. I shook too. It
taxied to the runway. It was taking off without Sidney
Poitier. But they had promised me. He would be there.
He would ride in. In a pumpkin seed. To take care of me.
To hold my hand. And when we land to dance me up the
Plantation stairs in Dem Golden Slippers. They'd lied. He
didn't show up. If my voices had lied about Sidney Poitier, then they could have lied about the plane's credentials. It wasn't smiling. It was smirking. Grinning. They
had tricked me again. Kill the priest! We're in danger!
Don't you understand, everybody! Kill the father! He
lied! Oh, God, we're going to crash!

3

It's all right, folks. She's only sick. Who was she talking about? Somebody must have diphtheria. Not me. She was smiling at me. A very nice stewardess. I was very grateful for her concern about my condition. I was pregnant with my first mother, Florence. Floss. Flo. I smiled back. Then I let her put my Protestant fur coat over my shoulders. She put it on backwards. To cover the Bare Breasts. Pink. Underdone. Not like Sidney Bojangles Poitier. He was nice and brown on the outside. Brother Coley the World War II pilot turned off the Gas. The plane stayed alive quite a while. Even with its head turned off. Then it stopped. Pan Am. Initials. Oh, God, I'm seeing them again. But you're too big for that stuff. I can't help H-E-L-P it. Okay. P-A-N. Papa. André. Nick. I took a deep breath to blow away the initials. The plane blew up. Explosion. Sirens. Ambulance. Speeding. Close Burma Shaves. Don't wave. The flags flew. High and free. It's the safest way. I promise you. It's the only way to fall. If I should wake before I die it's because I say sew. I see. I'se. Is. I. I staired inn two A-(n)-G-(e)-L ass Boo!

4

I stared into a glass booth. Somebody moved. Bless me, Father, for I have sinned. Would you please give me penance and absolution and tell me is this the Terminal Exit. The person turned. I saw me. In my white communion dress and Chantilly lace Veil. No, not me. A nurse. In a white uniform and cap. Not rolling bandages. Behind her was a picture. A beautiful building. Cul-ver Ci-ty Ho-SPIT-al. Culver City wasn't in London by the light of the silv'ry moon. Culver City was in Los Angeles. Good old City of the Angels. Right? Right. Hello, Mrs. Previn, Dory, nice to see you again. I waved to her. Hello. She came out of the glass booth. She took my arm and led me back down the corridor to my pew. I had on paper slippers. They kept sliding off. How the hell could I do my tap dance? I knew it would be nice here. But I had no idea it would be this nice. Could I please stay two weeks instead of one? Yes, if you don't try to flush yourself down the toilet again. She unlocked the room. There was no Christmas tree. She sat me down on the bed. Symptoms. I didn't want it but I took the pill. I always do as I'm told. Because I'm obedient. To my Superiors. Which means everybody. How come everybody else in the world seems to have it all together and can go everywhere and swallow pills without being terrified they'll choke to death? She watched with her terrible eye till it went down. Wintergreen. Past my tight throat. Into the orange pits. Where the palm tree grows. Into Dory. Into the clay pits. Where Dorothy grows. Upside down. To age ten. Dorothy never grows past age ten. She started growing upside down on her mama's living room floor. At about age three. She stopped growing in her father's dining room. At age ten. Then she came out. And she closed the door. And she started all over again. Back to age three. Once more. Up to age ten. Over again. Then she came out. And closed the door. Then she went back once more, and once more she says, please, leave on the light. I'm afraid of spiders. All right. Go to sleep. Good-night. But now the door is closed and locked from the outside. It doesn't matter. She's back. Inside. Alone. In solitude. In the lock. In her cell. Back where she belongs. Dorothy closed her eyes and smiled. I smiled, too. I was so happy. I didn't even get upset when somebody screamed. Screamed inside my empty cell. My Sterile cell. Cell. Sperm. Seed. Pits. Spit. Swallow. Eyes. Nose. Mouth. Hair. Heir. Air. Air plane. Air plain. Heir pain. Air plan. Air Pan. Peter Pan. Pan Am. Am pa. Our pa. Your pa. pa. pa . . .

5

my daddy says
i ain't his child
ain't that something
ain't that wild
daddy says
i ain't his child
ain't that something wild
my hair is curly
my freckles are tan
could my daddy be
the garbage man
my legs are stumpy
my fingers are short
like my uncle will
who is the bowling sport
my eyes are slanty
like mister woo
hey mister laundry man
is it you

i'm ugly as steve
with the big mustache
but mama says poles
are a piece of trash
my daddy says
i ain't his child
ain't that something
ain't that wild
daddy says
i ain't his child
ain't that something wild
hey anybody
i might have missed
would you care to state
that i exist
i ain't quite sure
what it is i did
to make him swear
that i ain't his kid
but he told mama
and she told me
back when i was
just about three
she felt my face
and she kind of smiled
and she said
he says
you ain't his child
my daddy says
i ain't his child
ain't that something
ain't that wild
daddy says i ain't his child
ain't that something wild

6

Not his kid? Well, if not his, then, I'd like to know, whose
the hell is she? My Toonerville Trolley went off its track.
The wheel broke and lay there. Spinning. On the Repeated Flo-ribunda Rose Pattern linoleum. How'd it happen so fast? There I was, one minute, playing with it on
Mama's living room floor. While her and Aunt Rose
talked and had coffee and crullers. And the next minute
everything came loose and fell apart. Broke. Beyond repair. No good. Not his? Well, really! I mean, he was always a liar, that brother of mine. Even when we were
kids. I'm gonna talk to that son-of-a-bitch, Florence. No,
Rose, please don't. For my sake. I'm the one's got to live
with him. I'm the one knows what he's capable of doing. I
walk around here on eggs. I'll take anything, just so's not
to set him off again. I can't go through that another time.
I won't, and that's that! I put the ruined Toonerville back
on the track. Hoping Mama hadn't noticed it breaking
while she talked. In the way adults have of doing two
things at the same time. I pushed it along the rest of the

Repeated Flo-ribunda Rose Pattern. The flower being the Main Street and the thorns being blocks. Just to finish the trip. But it was too late. The damage was done. A passenger could fall out and be dumped into the abandoned clay pits. Never to be heard from again. That trolley could never be trusted any more. Y'know, Florence, I remember once he broke his glasses. And for no reason, he lied all over the place. He kept swearing he didn't break them. But everybody knew he was full of shit. And would he change his story? Oh, no. Neither would he say he was sorry, I bet. Huh, Rose? He's never sorry for what he did. Well, no matter. I always say, God moves in strange ways, his punishment to perform. What I mean is, look at her, Rose. Don't she look like he spit her out of his mouth? Every time that man lays his eyes on her, what's he see? The spittin' image of himself. So don't you think that reminds him of how much he made me suffer? That's his cross and he has to bear it. Oh, he's mellowed. Since Dorothy started taking tap lessons, butter won't melt in his mouth. Now he acts like the sun rises and sets in her. The sun? Mama told me once that if I swallowed the pits an orange tree would grow in my stomach and that's bad enough. But the sun. Big. Burning. Like the Flaming Fires of Hell. Hell is a bad word to say. But, Florence, he can't just go around saying that terrible thing about his own child. Well, he hasn't actually said it in a long time. Not in so many words. Since he began to regard her as the apple of his eye, he'd just as soon forget it. But I don't forget. That's why, from time to time, I got to say it to someone in the family. Someone like you, Rose. I can keep it in just so long. Then it starts gnawin' at me. Once I let it out, I can swallow it again. Mama dunked a piece of cruller into her coffee and ate it. I threw the Toonerville across the floor. It hit the overstuffed mohair sofa. Bounced off one of the claw feet. And crashed upside

down against Aunt Rose's ankle. Dorothy! Say you're
sorry to your Aunt Rose, immediately, if not sooner! I'm
sorry, Aunt Rose. Well, you better be. That's okay, Dot.
All's you did was breaked the damned bone in two vital
places. What got into her, Rose? She's never unruly. I
hate an unruly, disobedient kid. Say it won't happen
again, Dorothy, what you did. I wasn't sure which one of
the things it was I did. But, okay. It won't happen again,
Aunt Rose. That's more like it. Now, put your toy away
like a good little girl. I picked up the toy and dropped it.
What's eating her, Rose? I don't know, d'you think she
heard, Florence? No. You know how it is with kids. Just
goes in one ear and out the other. Last stop, I said to myself. Real quiet. So as not to make any more waves or else
Mama would be sure to see the bad wheel and toys cost
good money. I put it into the drawer of the gate-legged
table. The one where we put all the broken stuff that
couldn't be used any more, but couldn't be thrown away
on account of costing good money. Things that can't
breathe are break-able. Like Mama's porcelain painted
saint. St. Francis of Assisi, who loves all animals. Can I
have a kitten, Mama? No. Can't you see we're still talking? I closed the drawer. Careful not to slam. I caught my
pinky. It smarted. I wanted to put it in my mouth and
suck on it. But I couldn't. Me being too big and it being
the left pinky and we all know which side the left is, don't
we? Just the same, Florence, I think I ought to say something to that bastard brother of mine. No, Rose, please.
He's my husband, for better, for worse, and I say, don't
make waves. Let sleeping dogs lay. I went over to a chair
and sat. I pulled my dress down over my knees. To show I
am modest. Mama smiled at Aunt Rose. Aunt Rose smiled
at Mama. I smiled at both of them. Because I am an obedient child. I am not my father's spit.

7

when i was a child
she taught me how
to turn the other cheek
never start a row she said
know when you shouldn't speak
listen dorothy
do be good
an obedient child behaves
bury your frown
down under the ground
and above all
don't make waves
that's how my mama
brought me up
and my mama gave me
good advice
here i am
i'm standin' right here
didn't i turn out nice

when i was a child
i sat so still
in my daddy's wicker chair
when company came
i was so good
they never knew i was there
listen dorothy
don't talk back
an obedient child behaves
bury your frown
down under the ground
and above all
don't make waves
that's how my mama
brought me up
and my mama gave me
good advice
here i am
i'm sittin' right here
didn't i turn out nice

when i was a child
i dutifully learned
to turn the other cheek
i swallowed my opinions whole
i knew when not to speak
now here i lie
beneath this stone
in one of the quieter graves
where my epitaph is carved:
she never did make waves
that's how my mama
brought me up
and my mama gave me

good advice
here i am
i'm lying right here
didn't i turn out nice

8

The dome ceiling was nearly as high as Heaven. All painted with glorious clouds. Surrounding a ring of silver light. And in the center of that light He sat. On a beautiful horse. Rudolph Valentino. Some dead Star from the Olden Days. His head glowed. His divine eyes looked up. His arm was stretched out. His perfect finger pointed down. Beneath him knelt the harem ladies. With peacock-feather fans and sequined veils and diamond crosses around their necks. Their hands reached out to his Wondrous Presence. Towards the vicinity of his loins. But they weren't able to touch his loins. The harem ladies were too far beneath him. They weren't even able to touch his horse's loins. That's how far below the ladies were. Outside the silver ring was a desert scene. Palm trees with spangled coconuts and pasted-on gaudy green leaves. Real different from the dried-up stalks that the altar boys passed out on Palm Sunday. But they must all come from the same place. Some exotic island where they dined on mince and slices of quince where Baby Jesus was born.

Mama, they spelled Holy wrong. Where, Dot? On the ceiling. Oh, that don't spell Holy. That spells Holly. Like in Christmas? No, like in Hollywood. Now, stop asking questions and get into your costume. The other kids are all dressed. You're acting kind of sluggish, are you okay? Yes, Mama. I was roasting, but I was scared to tell. I looked at the radiator. The arrow pointed to Min. Heat. The other side of Max. Heat. Min was Marie Dressler, Daddy's favorite lady movie star. She lived in Hollywood with Fred Astaire. Once I saw her picture in a magazine. Swimming in her own swimming pool. I wished I could swim. I followed Mama out of the dressing room. Someday I was gonna go out to Hollywood to live and have a maid. Daddy promised if I practiced real hard he'd take me there to be in the movies. And I believed him. He was waiting for me at the bottom of the spiral steps. He looked right past Mama. Up at me. In my two-piece costume and Spanish shawl. He smiled. So nice and friendly. I wondered what he did to Mama. That she couldn't go through it again. He could never do anything wrong. He was too handsome. With the stage lights shining, like Rudolph's silver ring, around the rim of his glasses. The whole effect made me dizzy. I was starting to sweat. He reached up. How do I look, Daddy? I started down. The heel of my tap shoe got caught. I pitched forward and fell into his arms. Daddy was always there to catch me. Mama frowned. Careful of your fringe! I'm sorry, Mama. You look just swell, Dot. Thank you, Daddy. You got a good luck kiss for me? I stood on my tip-toes. He turned his face to one side, like always. And I planted a kiss on his right cheek. I got a whiff of Old Spice After-Shave. It was a real occasion, he was wearing a tie. His one and only best. His last year's birthday present from me. I was glad he was wearing my present and not somebody else's. Mama always gave him a leatherette change purse. But you couldn't see a leatherette change purse. I don't know what made me trip and fall on you, Daddy. I'm clumsy. Maybe you need glasses, Dot, like me. Glasses? Then I'd really look like I'm your little girl, wouldn't I, Daddy? He didn't answer. Mama sucked phlegm from her sinuses and swallowed. Then she shoved me hard. Like I said something wrong. What'd I say, Mama? Did I say something wrong? No! And I didn't pay good money for lessons to have you miss your performing debut. Now get out there! I looked at Daddy. He nodded. I ran onto the stage. And took my place. At the end of the line. I was always the shortest kid. Under the lights was even hotter. Inside my head was a blur. How would I remember my steps? They were all mixed up. Waltz-clog, buck and wing, shuffle-ball-change, trenches and turkey-trot. Oh God-in-Your-Infinite-Mercy, grant me the power to be good. I have to be for my father because I love him and for my mother because she paid good money for this. I clasped my hands together. The music started. I looked upwards. The curtain opened. Again. I saw the dome ceiling. Oh, my God! Rudolph's finger was pointing right in my direction. His burning eyes stared down at me. The silver ring had turned to gold. Like the broiling Hollywood sun. Rays of fire shot out from the edges. Like the Flaming Fires of Hell. The horse rose up. Its red-hot metal hooves flashed over my head. Like pokers. The horse whinnied. Rudolph Valentino laughed. The pokers came crashing down on me. The ceiling spun. And the sun exploded.

9

The chicken pox lasted a long time. Mama made me wear white cotton gloves. But I managed to scratch anyway. Leaving three pockmarks Mama said I'd carry to my grave. My fever was a hundred-and-five degrees and for two-and-a-half days I was Intermittently Delirious. Last night I had this bad dream, Daddy. I dreamed that Mickey Mouse was coming up from the cellar with a hatchet. And he was gonna chop my head off. My father laughed so hard tears came down his cheeks. He took off his silver-rimmed bifocals and wiped them clean with the bib of his Sears Catalog overalls. I took my chance and stole a peep at his bare eye. There was no apple. So how could he forget, Mama? Forget what, Dot? She must be Inter-mittently Delirious again. No, Mama, I'm not being Inter-mittently Delirious again. You said Daddy was being punished 'cause he spit me out of his mouth. And now you said he was trying to forget that since I became the apple of his eye. But there's no apple. Is there, Daddy? Daddy got up real fast and stomped down the stairs to the cellar. Mama put a wet cloth over my face. Mama? Forget it, Dorothy. The house was already too hot, so I didn't know why Daddy was stoking the furnace again. But we both heard him down there. Loud. Like he was hitting it or something. Mama? I said forget it. I was just gonna ask you why my left eye is smaller than my right eye. Mama lifted the cloth from my face. She stared at me for a few minutes. Because that's the way you were born, Dorothy. See, everybody comes into this world with one angel side and one devil side. The angel side is the right side, of course. The devil side is the left. And that's why your left eye is smaller. That and The Veil. Thirty-three long hours I was in labor. I pushed so hard. I screamed so loud, I almost choked on my own tongue. From time to time, the nuns would moisten my mouth with Canada Dry. And I thanked them. But I couldn't even keep down Canada Dry. No wonder. With you in there. Crowding me. It was almost like you were refusing to come out. The Doctor, he told me you'd be out by the twentieth. The twenty-first at the latest. But you stayed in there till the twenty-second. At five minutes past the stroke of midnight they pulled you out with instruments. You must have put up a terrible fight. You were full of bruises. And so ugly! With that Veil draped over your left eye. Like one of Myrna Loy's hats. That eye stayed swelled up and shut tight. Even after they cut away the Veil. That's why your middle name is Veronica. Your Aunt Mamie and me, we waited till Daddy was at work. Then we actually sneaked you into the house. I don't give a damn if that bastard's in the house, he said. Just so long as I don't have to lay eyes on her. Before you were born, I secretly sewed your layette. Pink. I was so sure you'd be a girl. At night when he left for work, I'd take that layette out and unfold every piece. And I'd think, well, if nobody wants her but me, then she's mine. Alone. My gift. From

God. That's why I called you Dorothy. Down at the five
and dime there was this book of first names. It was too expensive to buy. So I went through it till I came to
Dorothy. Gift of God. I originally wanted to call you
Eileen. But just before I went to the Hospital I read in
the paper that Eileen Langan, aged three, had died.
Causes unknown. Did I tell you that? Yes, Mama, you
told me that. And every time we rode to Perth Amboy on
the Number Three bus, and we passed the cemetery,
she'd point it out. The grave. Langan, it said, but no relation. It wasn't the usual kind of stone. It was a small marble house. A house is a place where a person lives. A
house isn't a grave. It was the first time I ever heard of a
little child being buried in a house. I couldn't understand
it. But the next time I heard of it, I understood.

10

I never saw you walk on eggs, Mama. Would you do it for me? What're you talking about, Dot? The way you have to walk so as not to set Daddy off again. Oh, that was just a figure of speech, Dot. Well, what could Daddy have done to you that was so terrible? Forget it, Dorothy. You don't forget, do you, Mama? No, I don't forget. I swallow it. And that's what I want you to do. From now on, when you start to wonder what it was that Daddy did to me, you just swallow the thought. You hear? Yes, Mama, I hear. Mama? What now, Dot? I was just wondering. What if it won't go down?

11

tomorrow is thanksgiving
and i'm as glad as glad can be
for i'll have
a piece of the turkey
that used to gobble at me.

I stood on one of the dining room chairs. So I could look
out the window. And see it doing its turkey trot. It was
the first live bird we ever had. Mama never won anything. But this was the second prize. She bought one raffle
ticket and forgot about it till it was left on the doorstep.
For the benefit of the Missionary priests in Mainland
China. Once Mama took me to eat Chinese Food. In New
York. Where my Grandma and Grandpa Shannon lived.
That was the best dinner I ever had. I only really like
vegetables. With space between them. If the juice from
my buttered carrots touches my mashed potatoes I get
nauseous. And then Mama makes me leave the table and
go into the bathroom to sit. With my head on the sink.

Till my stomach stops rumbling and my hands stop sweating. That's how much I hate to see my vegetables touch. I also hate wings of turkey and drumsticks of turkey. I only eat white meat. Even with its head chopped off it stayed alive. For quite a while. I didn't want to hear that. Your father and I watched it run all over the blessed yard. I wished I could put my hands over my ears. Once it tripped over its own noggin. If you can picture that image. Image. I could change the subject. What's A Image, Mama? Not A Image, Dot. *An* Image. Ann Image? Spit Ann Image? I was really mixed up now. But I didn't want to ask her that one and make waves. She plucked the feathers and singed the stubble with a candle. She stuffed it. Stale bread and port wine. Does Daddy know about the port wine, Mama? Shit! She pricked her finger with the needle. She washed off the blood and finished sewing up the hole. She tied the twine in a bow and sprinkled the flesh with salt, pepper, and Gold Medal Flour. She crossed the legs modestly and she bound them together. Then she pinned the wings behind its back. Actually, she only pinned one wing. The left wing had already been broken and lost. Some neighborhood cat must have made off with it. Are birds right-winged or left-winged? I wanted to ask her but she hadn't answered the port wine question, what with pricking her finger at the exact same moment. So I opened the oven door for her and she shoved the pale bird inside. Then she closed the door and turned up the gas. What a mess this kitchen is! I wondered why she said that so loud. I'm just going to put everything away so it'll be nice and neat for dinner. Was she talking to somebody in the other room? She picked up the bottle of port wine and went into the pantry. I waited to help her straighten up. But she stayed in there a long time. I called. She didn't answer. I didn't go in. I left the kitchen. I was glad to get out of having to help. I was outside when I heard the crash. Breaking glass. Maybe she cut herself again. I pretended I didn't hear.

12

We give thanks, Oh Lord, for these our blessings and for
Thy gifts which we are about to receive. Amen. Amen.
Amen. My father stood at the head of the table, sharpen-
ing his knife. Scrape. Scrape. Some people eat to live, as
they say. Me, I live to eat. I know you do, Mike. Sure
smells good. Dorothy, don't it smell good? Yes, Mama. I
hope it's done enough, Flo. Oh, it's done, Mike. It's done.
Her words were a bit slurred. The scrape scraping
stopped. He tested the knife with his thumb. His nail was
split down the center. What's in the dressing, Flo? The
usual, Mike. Stale bread and sage. Chopped parsley and a
pinch of thyme. That all? That's all. He looked at her. She
took my plate quick and stacked it on hers. When she set
them in front of him they clattered. Look how nice and
brown the outside is. Done to a turn. The outside don't
mean a blessed thing, Flo. The bird could still be underdone on the inside and you know how I am about fowl
that's pink. I know, Mike. It won't be pink. I'll take the
dark meat. And leave the rest for you two. Your father's

just like you, Dot. Like father, like daughter. He'll only eat the breast. He in-serted the knife. The skin burst. Juice oozed out of the crack. It rolled over the blade edge. Down the thighs of the crossed legs. And dripped onto the platter. He went in again. On an angle. Across the breast. The outer crust fell away. The inner meat showed. A little blue bruise marked the off-center cut. He slammed the tools on the table. Son of a Bitch! What, Mike? You know what! I cooked it four-and-a-half hours, didn't I, Dot? I never left the kitchen, did I? Tell your father. Tell me shit! But Mike, it's a twelve-pound bird. That's twenty minutes to the pound. No, that's thirty minutes to the pound. Let me see. Thirty minutes at approximately 350 is—Twenty, thirty, the bastard is pink! I'll put it back in the oven, Mike. You'll put nothing back! *I'll* put it! Where it *belongs!* The chair fell as she got up. She tried to beat him to the bird but he already had it. She reached out and grabbed. He pulled it away. Juice ran over their hands. They struggled. As they tore across the room. Tugging at the bird. Slipping and sliding in the grease of the spilled gravy. They looked like skaters in a Sonja Henie movie.

13

Grandma Langan's name was Ann and she ironed. Uncle Nick's wife was also Ann and she was a telephone operator. Then there was my other aunt. She spelled it with an E. Aunt Anne had reddish hair like mine. After she had her baby in the Ho-spit-al she was sitting up in a chair. The nurse came in. Are you all right, Missus? She said, I'm fine, Nurse. And she smiled. And turned her head. And died. I went to her funeral. My first one. I wore a new pink dress with blue stripes across the front. And a bow that tied in the back. One of the few times Mama ever bought new for me. On account of the Depression. Most of my wardrobe was picked up at old rummage stores and fire sales. And worst of all, Mama was a garbage picker. I didn't mind the rummage clothes or the fire sale close-outs. But I was always scared of going some place and have some kid look at me. And say, what are you doing in my old dress? That I threw into the garbage? That dress is three years old. Only three? In our house, garbage meant the end of the line. Something had

to go a whole lot longer than three years in our house before it qualified as garbage. Eggshells and orange rinds.
Stuff that couldn't be reboiled for soup. Or reheated for
stew. And this was certainly the first time I'd ever seen
anything thrown out in our house while it could still be
put to good use. I tried to picture the Image of Tom Turkey. Yesterday. In the backyard. Doing his comical trot. I
looked at Tom Turkey. Today. Thrown out because he
was pink. He lay on his side. His recent breast surgery
wasn't visible. But the broken left wing was all jagged. I
felt as bad as bad could be. I wanted a piece of the turkey
that used to gobble at me. But, as Daddy always said, if
he don't eat, nobody eats. The broken wing looked so
bare. I reached down for some wilted parsley. I came up
with the port wine bottle. It was empty. I pushed it down
to the bottom of the garbage. I covered the broken wing
with the wilted parsley. I left the kitchen. I went up the
stairs to the bedroom and knocked on the door. Go away.
Her words were even more slurred than at the table. She
gagged. Then she spit up the Green Bile. After the Green
Bile she'll be De-pressed. That's the way it works. I used
to think being De-pressed meant not being ironed. That's
why I asked Grandma Langan. No, Dorothy. Being De-
pressed means getting the Blues. How do you get the
Blues, Grandma? From missing somebody. Like somebody's father? Yes. Or from losing something. Like your
eyesight? Or the use of your right hand. Or the use of
your left hand? No, not your left hand so much. Like my
helium balloon that went up into the sky over Maple
Street? Like that, Grandma? Yes, Dorothy, like that. The
next Thanksgiving Mama invited an old acquaintance
from her girlhood, Ceil Casey. I couldn't figure out why.
She never talked much about Ceil Casey. And we never
had company for dinner. We couldn't ever chance it with
Daddy's temper going off you never knew when. But

Mama put her foot down. She wasn't going to cook a whole turkey and trimmings. Not unless there was someone there to share in the festivities. About your friend, Ceil Casey. Does she drink, Flo? No, Mike. My friend Ceil Casey is a teetotaler. Just like you. What an enchanting little child you have, Florence. Such a dear thing. Thank you, Ceil. And so well-mannered. Say thank you, Dorothy. Thank you, Aunt Ceil. You're most certainly welcome, Dorothy. My most certainly welcome wore out real fast. At the dinner table the dear thing devoured everything in sight. After two huge helpings of turkey, the dear thing picked at the scraps. Tore meat from the breast bone. And snatched the last piece of white meat from the platter. Before her father could get to it. Mama was absolutely flabbergasted and the old acquaintance had second thoughts. Her description of my behavior went downhill from dear thing to revoltingly rude. I had never been called rude in my entire life. I couldn't imagine what had gotten into me. I hated myself. And I couldn't stop myself from spoiling such perfect festivities. Where the stuffing was moistened with giblet broth instead of port wine. And the white meat was done to a turn. Without a trace of the dreaded pink. Without being sent, I took myself off to the bathroom. To sit in disgrace with my sweating head on the sink. I never felt so nauseous. That was the funny thing. I hadn't even wanted all that turkey. I couldn't understand why I'd made such a pig of myself. What do you suppose got into me, Daddy? I don't know, pal. Here, take this Ex-Lax. I didn't want Ex-Lax. I didn't want anything ever again. I took it and forced it into my mouth. It had a taste of decay. Maybe it's poisoned, Daddy. It's not poisoned, I promise you. That made me feel better. I swallowed it and went upstairs to lay me down to sleep. I prayed the Lord my soul to keep. But I knew I would not die before I wake. The

Lord wouldn't come, my soul to take because Daddy said Ex-Lax wasn't poisoned. And when Daddy told me something, I believed him. Up until then. But that Thanksgiving with the old acquaintance was the last. The next Thanksgiving never happened. Neither did Hallowe'en or my birthday or Christmas or New Year's. That next year was when I learned that a house could be a grave. And that somebody could be buried alive.

14

in my sweet little
alice blue gown
when i first wandered
down into town
i was both proud and shy
as i felt every eye
and in every shop window
i primped passing by
then in manner of fashion
i frowned
and the world
seemed to smile
all around
till it wilted i wore it
i'll always adore it
my sweet little
alice blue gown

15

My performing debut was postponed more than a whole year. And it didn't take place in Elizabeth in the big city movie house with the Hollywood dome ceiling, either. It went on right at home, in the drab, beige-painted State Theater in Woodbridge where every Saturday matinee they had dishes and a double feature, followed by a live show. Supplied by the local Academy of the Art of the Dance. A chorus of six, wearing silver Capezio tap shoes with heels and grosgrain ribbons and costumes of black sateen flared-bottom pants. And blue sateen blouses with big Peter Pan collars and floppy bows. And shiny cardboard tophats and we all got to wear lipstick, Tangee natural. As usual, I was the last kid on the end. So it was easy for me to steal away from the group. I went behind the screen. For this particular Special Kiddies' Attraction they were showing *Cinderella*. Giant shadows moved. Dancing with other giant shadows. The screen wasn't silver. It was drab gray. With thousands of tiny threads connected to one another. Here and there a thread was broken. It must have been from the weight of all those giants dancing. The scene was in the ballroom of the castle. But it wasn't at all the same as when you saw it from the other side. Prince Charming's charming talk sounded like stupid gibberish. Cinderella's adorable face was covered with pockmarks. The king's royal musicians were playing backwards. Everything was blurred. The entire congregation acted confused and out of control. I couldn't believe my eyes. Big important giants dancing around, bumping into each other, like a bunch of clumsy kids playing Blind-Man's Buff. I laughed at the crazy sight and I was sad. I wanted those movie stars to get back to their former neatness and glamor. The way they acted when I sat out in the audience. Staring up at them. Eating my Necco wafers in the dark. I mean, how could I be sure who I was, if they weren't sure who they were? The Prince gargled some words of love. Cinderella gave him a crooked kiss. And ꓷИƎ ƎHT flashed across their fading faces. The piano player in the pit struck up a chord. The spotlight hit. And I ran back to my place in the line and followed after the other kids. Smiling and tapping. As though nothing happened. Like I'd never left the group. And stolen a terrible glimpse behind the big screen.

16

I never could get my body off the ground. No Hands.
That's what it was called in Acrobatic Class. There I
stood attached to the floor. While the other kids lifted
themselves up and hurled their bodies into the air. I could
do somersaults better than anybody. Cartwheels, headstands, fish flops. I could even cross my hands over my
chest, go into a backbend, and pick up a handkerchief
with my teeth. But I couldn't make my body fly. I
couldn't make it float either. Once in Lake Hopatcong,
Daddy threw me off the dock. Sink or swim. I chose sink.
They pulled me out. Purple and sputtering. Just like out
from under the kitchen faucet when I had the Convulsions. Every night, at twelve midnight, this child here
wakes up in Convulsions. Tell me what to do, Doctor. I
mean, this child here screams so long her eyes roll back in
her head and she turns purple and her breath stops. I pick
her up from her crib and hold her and walk with her but
nothing stops her tears. I'm afraid this child here is liable
to choke to death. The doctor had a good prescription.

The first night this child here woke up screaming, Mama picked her up and, per his orders, carried her to the kitchen sink, turned on the cold water full blast, and stuck her head under the faucet. She hated to do it, but I was already at the purple stage so what could she lose? I was in a rage. But then I must have been in an out-rage. I sputtered and choked and screamed. Finally I stopped. The second night, I sputtered and choked. The third night, I sputtered. After two weeks of the nightly remedy, I stopped altogether. From time to time, I woke up crying after that, but the minute my mother came near the crib, before she even tried to pick me up, she said I would change, just like that. Into obedient silence. The good doctor's prescription was a complete success. There was no more screaming. For the time being.

17

'member the way
i used to time step
lord it made him proud
he told his friends
(he never told me)
that i stood above the crowd

Mistake. Everytime he caught me, that's what he'd yell.
And I'd jump. I used to get so nervous waiting for that
word I'd forget my routine. Then he'd get up and try to
show me where I was wrong. He loved to help me practice. He'd balance my feet for my headstands. He'd support my spine for my handsprings. He'd weigh me down
to stretch my inner thighs for splits. And when my daily
hour was over he'd get out this drugstore stuff. It was
white but it was called cocoa butter. And he'd massage
me. He'd scoop up that cocoa butter between his hands
and he'd rub it into my legs. At first he'd rub fast. Then
he'd slow down. And I'd watch him. Following the

rhythm of his motion. After a while he'd get all dreamy. So would I. Sometimes I couldn't tell where his skin stopped and my skin started. Then I'd close my eyes. But instead of relaxing, my breath would start to go faster. For some reason, that made me feel funny. So I'd jump up like I thought he was finished rubbing me. And I'd run all over the house. Looking and looking till I found Mama. Can I sit on your lap and you sing to me like you used to? Oh Dot, you're getting too big for that sort of thing. Besides, your father's taken over that stuff with you. He has not taken over that stuff with me! What's the matter, Dot? Nothing's the matter. Have you got a fever? Your face is all hot. It isn't hot. All right, you big mope, come on. Climb on my lap. You smell like fudge. It's the cocoa butter. How can something smell like chocolate and not be dark, Mama? Hushabye, my little pick-aninny, sandman's gonna get you if you don't. I mean, don't you think? If something smells like cocoa and is named cocoa, don't you think it couldn't be white? Hushabye, hushabye, mammy's little baby. Mammy's little coal black rose. Don't you think, Mama? What, Dorothy? That I'm plain? Or do you think I'm pretty? I think you're plain *and* pretty. But every old crow thinks its own's as white as snow. How come nobody has freckles around here but me? I don't know. I asked Daddy where they came from. What did he say? Keep rocking, Mama. What did your father say? He said I got them from the fly on the wall. They're flyspecks, pal, is what he said. Don't you cry, my little pick-aninny, don't you mind what the white folks say. They forgot to give your mammy a talcum powder shammy. But you're mammy's little coal black rose. He calls me pal. That's nice.

18

There are two things that mean the Big Time Show Business. New York City and the *Billboard* Magazine. That's what Daddy always said. When the new issue arrived in the mailbox, he'd take it into the kitchen and he'd sit with it for hours at the porcelain enameled table. He always read every single page. Every announcement for a carnival show or a circus. Every Going-Broke sale. Every bubble gum dis-penser, pawned instrument, and pinball machine. This is my bible, he used to say. But he never seemed to find anything he wanted. Until we opened the lunchroom on account of the Depression. Then he found just the right slot machine. Also, there was the Marxaphone. The advertisement proudly stated that this instrument was one of a kind. Actually invented by one of the four Marx Brothers. Daddy sent away for one. It arrived with no instructions for how to play it. So we sent away for a booklet. Our letter was returned. The company had gone out of business. Nobody ever did figure out how to play that Marxaphone and Daddy knew we'd gotten stuck. But he chalked it up to experience. Mama was beginning to complain about the investment. And Daddy was beginning to get discouraged. But one day the entire subscription paid itself off. When he came across the ad for the auditions. Children were being picked for New York City radio programs.

RADIO PERFORMER
DOROTHY LANGAN
Woodbridge. Miss Dorothy Langan, daughter of Mr. and Mrs. Michael Langan, of town, made a successful radio debut, Sunday morning from 9 A.M. to 10 A.M. on the "Rainbow Hour" over station WOR.
The local youngster sang "Yankee Doodle Never Went to Town." She had two successful radio auditions before her appearance Sunday and may be kept on as a steady feature on the program if she obtains enough votes by mail.
—*Woodbridge Independent*

I wasn't kept on as a steady feature on that program. I didn't get enough votes. My next big chance was to be on the Major Bowes Amateur Hour. Daddy carefully selected my song and every day for a month he rehearsed me, even though Mama mentioned several times how the front lawn was starting to look neglected. Daddy had to stay with the store so Mama got to take me on the Jersey Central into New York City. Daddy had a radio plugged in behind the counter and made a couple of customers who were sitting at one of the three tables shut up so he could hear me sing. Later I heard one of the customers tell Mama that Daddy kept saying I was his. That's my kid, he kept saying, that's my kid. Just like in that Wallace Beery movie. Of course, everybody else in the picture knew Wallace Beery was lying. Everybody but Jackie Cooper.

19

i'm shootin' high
got my eye
on a star
in the sky
shootin' high
i'll never stop
till i get
to the top
tell me why

A little girl with long silky straight brown hair and pink
rosettes and a crepe-de-chine accordian-pleated dress
sang "Mighty Lak a Rose" and won the Major Bowes
Amateur Hour. All the way home on the train Mama kept
saying how good that little girl was with the straight
brown hair. "Mighty Lak a Rose" was her idea of a perfect selection. But nobody had ever asked her for her
opinion. She never mentioned my rendition of "Shootin'
High." Daddy said that I did just fine. And that he wasn't

the least bit mad or disappointed. But he issued a Boy-cott. From then on we were forbidden to listen to the Major Bowes Amateur Hour. And he also cancelled his subscription to the *Billboard* Magazine.

20

NEWSETTES:

Dorothy (well-known local entertainer) Langan appears Saturday and Sunday evenings with Ken Stoe's Blue Terrace Orchestra at Block's Popular Grove.

—*Woodbridge Independent*

Four dollars per show is what they paid me. Added to the lunchroom's take, the money I earned meant the difference between a good week and a bad one. I was the Opening Act at Block's Popular Grove. The one that warmed up the audience for the Main Attraction. Daddy wasn't too crazy about that. But he thought it might lead to bigger things. Meanwhile, I was getting good experience. Up till then I'd only appeared with other kids. But this Main Attraction was a real Professional. A Hawaiian dancer from Long Beach, California. Glamorous as Dorothy Lamour. She gave me permission to watch her put on her Professional makeup in the ladies' restroom. I felt honored. After she finished with pancake and rouge, lipstick and shadow, she took this black wax and she melted it in a spoon. Then she took a cardboard matchstick and she carefully applied one black wax bead to the tip of each and every one of her eyelashes. Top and bottom. When she finished, her eyes looked like twin black pearls. I asked Mama if she'd let me put on some mascara. Mama said absolutely not. I went out onto the floor of Block's Popular Grove feeling very drab. But I did the best I could under the circumstances. I finished my number and came off to a pretty fair round of applause considering that my eyes were so plain and that the audience was just marking time till they got to the Main Attraction. And then, the big moment came. Ken Stoe's Blue Terrace Orchestra went into the strains of "Sweet Leilani." The Main Attraction patted me on the head. An amber spot went on. And I watched her dance into the light. My scalp tingled where she'd touched me. Did you ever meet anybody like her before, Mama? I seen a lot like her before, Dorothy. Didn't her eyes look like twin pearls? More like twin spiders. But they were so shiny and glossy. Shiny and glossy, in my opinion, from a combination of Murine and straight gin. Was that a real gardenia in her hair? Yes, but the grass skirt was cellophane. I wonder if it's fireproof? I suddenly got panicked. What if some man with a big five-cent cigar made her go up in flames? I longed to be sure she was safe. I wanted to watch her. But I wasn't allowed. For my own good, Mama thought it best that I didn't see.

21

in the veterans' big parade
marched the businessmen's brigade
while behind the high school band
the ladies' fife and drum corps played
in the veterans' big parade
the flag flew high and free
down they marched to fourth and main
our soldiers died but not in vain
god was with us
that's for sure
he proved it 'cause
it didn't rain
balloons batons you wanted to cry
the best day in july

at the veterans' cemetery
then the services were said
and the mayor's first assistant
wiped his glasses

put them on
and read
ba ba ba ba ba
ba ba ba ba ba
we're gathered here
dear friends today
to show our brave boys
where they lay
we are with them all the way
and i think it's safe to say
they are not
alone
all the widows proudly smiled
(except for one with an infant child)
picnic time was then announced
and all the little kids went wild
picnic blankets then were spread
and the beer flowed fast and free
there were clams and corn on the cob
to feed the celebrating mob
(once in a while
i don't know why
the infant child
began to sob)
other than that it was new year's eve
till it was time to leave

then a fine hawaiian band
played and sang
aloha oe
and their voices drifted low
between the crosses
painted white
row on row on row
aloha oe

and so goodbye
till next year boys
next july
we are with you
all the way
and i think
it's safe to say
you are not
alone . . .

22

The Trouble started when Mama climbed up on a beer barrel and did a hula dance. All the lady friends looked at one another. And all the men laughed. All but Daddy. He was beet red in his American Legion Hat. With the Post Commander button. He led the parade down Main to the White Church cemetery off Rahway Avenue. He stood up on the platform. And gave his carefully memorized address. Then there was the annual presentation by Harry Fedderson of the traditional Lincoln's Gettysburg Address. Followed by me. Reading a patriotic poem. *In Flander's Field the poppies grow, between the crosses row on row that mark our place.* The mayor sent his best wishes in a telegram. Read aloud by the first assistant. The brave boys who gave their lives at the front received a three-gun salute from The Guard of Honor. After that, Daddy gravely held his hand over his heart, and gravely requested one minute of grave silence. The serious business of the day was concluded. And the picnic went ahead full steam. Clams. Corn on the cob. Orange Crush and Moxie. And all the beer you could drink. And that's what started the Trouble. See, Mama had this thing about al-co-hol. She would not touch the stuff. Unless it was around. And then she would not stay away from it. If there was a bottle anywhere in the vicinity she wasn't able to stop till she polished it off. But she always swore she wasn't the Drinking Type. And to prove the point she never brought anything into the house. Unless there was a Good Reason. Sweating out a cold was a Good Reason. Stuffing a turkey used to be a Good Reason. First Rate reasons were picnics. There she was protected from my father's anger by the other picnickers. Some of them actually encouraged her. Get up there, Florence. And get hot! They helped her onto the beer barrel. The Hawaiian band playing "Aloha Oe" in a real slow tempo suddenly went into "Back in Nagasaki, where the fellas chew tobaccy and the women wicky-wacky woo." And Mama went to town. She sings. She dances. She wiggles on her belly like a rep-tile! She lifted her flower print skirt up to her thighs and someone slapped Daddy on the back. Your wife sure is one hell of a good sport, Mike! Mike went red again and I turned away and ran from the hell of a good sport. I didn't stop till I came to the cemetery's civilian section. All the an-cest-ors. I wondered if I had any relatives buried there. I began to search frantically for my grandfather's grave. Nicholas Langan, loyal husband. Loving father. Why did they make up all that complimentary stuff about people when they were dead? As though they never lied to you when they were alive? Or never drank al-co-hol? Wouldn't it be funny if just once they carved the truth about adults? Just once, boy, I'd like to see a gravestone tell it right. Nicholas Langan, who beat up his son Mickey for accidentally breaking his expensive glasses. I walked past a grassy mound. There was an empty Budweiser bottle and half a clamshell. I picked up the shell. One side was rough. And gray as the stones that mark our place. I turned it over in my hand. The inner side was pearly pure and smooth as a rosary bead. I ran my finger over the silky surface. How could something so ugly on the outside be so pretty on the inside? It didn't make sense. Once I was running my finger over one of Daddy's unplaned two by fours. I asked him what the dark spots were. He said they were the knots. How could the straight surface feel rough and splintery and the tangled knots feel smooth and beautiful? The world was full of riddles and lies. I'd reached the far side of the cemetery. A couple of people were wondering. Was that Mrs. Michael Langan up there in the distance doing a hula on a beer barrel? They weren't asking me. I answered then anyway. No, that wasn't Mrs. Michael Langan up there doing a hula on a beer barrel. I was a liar. Bad as the rest of them. You couldn't believe anybody. I held the seashell to my ear. Of course, there was no sound of the ocean. I never heard of a person finding a pearl either. But a part of me still hoped. I dug a hole and buried the shell. The band finished "Back in Nagasaki." They went back into "Aloha Oe." I headed back the way I came. The beer bottle was still there. I kicked it hard. It rolled down the grassy mound and broke against a stone. Maybe it was my grandfather's stone. Maybe it wasn't my grandfather's.

. . . and their voices
drifted low
between the crosses
painted white
row on row on row
ba ba ba ba ba
ba ba ba ba ba
aloha oe

and so good-bye
till next year boys
next july
we are with you
all the way
and i think it's
safe to say
you are not alone
you are not alone

23

CROW'S NEST
BY THE NAVIGATOR

Little Dorothy Langan appeared in a local floor
show last night and received a big hand from the
audience. The girl is destined to reach greater
heights in the theatrical world.
—*Woodbridge Independent*

People were throwing money at me. All around me coins
were falling. Clinking and clattering at my feet. Nickels,
dimes, pennies, a few quarters, even a fifty-cent piece or
two. There was a big fat MC lady. Wearing a black velvet
ribbon around her throat and a wrist corsage. She shouted
at the customers. Calling them suckers. And I was pelted
by a fresh batch of coins. I turned to find Mama. She had
a surprised mortified look. But she just stood there. And I
felt like something you win at a pitch-a-penny stand in
Atlantic City. Finally, Mama got over her abashment. She
frantically waved for me to leave the stage. But the big

fat MC lady went over and told her not to be such a tight-ass. That was good money. Thrown to show genuine appreciation for the little lady's talent. Mama wasn't convinced about the genuine appreciation. No child of hers was going to go down on her knees in the dirt! What dirt? It's a clean Johnson-waxed floor! Get back out there, kid. Pick 'em up. You earned them. They're yours. But she's a child. She's a trouper! How about it folks! Ain't she a great little trouper? Scattered applause. I looked at Mama again. She didn't nod but she didn't say no. Slowly, I stooped to pick up a nickel. The applause got louder. I hesitated, then I picked up a couple of the bigger coins. One or two more were tossed. One hit me in the side and rolled under a table. I crawled underneath and came up with it. The crowd laughed. I scurried back and forth. The crowd egged me on. There! There's one! Get it! Get it! I had all of them but a fifty-cent piece. I dove under a chair for it. Suddenly Mama yanked me off and shoved me ahead of her. So hard I dropped some of the money. The MC lady howled. She wasn't too proud. She bent over for the fifty-cent piece. A man sitting behind her lifted up her skirt. She whirled on him. And pretended to slap his face. A flower from her wrist corsage fell between his legs. The audience roared. Mama hustled me fast into the dressing room. We were counting the money when the MC lady came in and threw us three more dimes, a couple of pennies, and four nickels, bringing the entire take to a grand total of five dollars and twenty-three cents. Not counting the half-dollar. More than I'd ever earned before. After that night, whenever they threw money, Mama let me pick it up. But she made me promise never to tell Daddy. Sometimes I'd miss a coin and she'd smile. A little embarrassed. And she'd point it out from the sidelines. Then she'd watch me while I went after it.

24

When Mama was a little girl who lived in the Bronx, the family couldn't afford to spend good money on fuel to heat their house. So every day during the winter months her mother would send her out to the Hudson River. There she'd search for scraps that were left behind by the unloading of the coal barges. Sometimes she'd find enough pieces to heat their freezing kitchen for a whole day. She used to gather the coal in her mother's apron that she wore over her older sister's last year's coat. When she found all the coal she could, she'd run home. Fast. So she wouldn't bump into other kids. If a couple did come along she'd turn away and pretend to look in store windows, hiding herself, so other kids couldn't see her black front and call her Coal-picker. Sometimes, I thought about when she used to stand on the river banks. Watching those soot-black ships. Heading out for other ports. Did she ever dream those ships were sailing away for a year and a day to some nice warm exotic island? Where they dined on mince and slices of quince? Where royal princesses danced the hula by the light of the silv'ry moon? To the land where the Bong-Tree grows?

25

shoeshine
five cents, sir
buy one if you can
for pa is dead
and ma has said
i now must be a man
shoeshine
said he
and did not see
the truck
that came his way
and while near death
with his last breath
these words
i heard him say
shoeshine
five cents, sir
buy one if you can
for pa is dead

and ma has said
i now must be a man

What d'you think of it, pal? Something I wrote for you.
What they call special material. After you do your verse
and chorus of "Shoeshine Boy," you recite this that I
wrote. You're dressed up like a little colored kid, see, with
a pair of my old cut-down black pants, a striped suspender, and a cap pulled over one eye. You're carrying
something I'm making for you right now down in the cellar. A shoeshine box. That's called a prop. A prop tells the
audience right away who you are and where you came
from. You get it? A shoeshine box for a shoeshine boy. It
sets the stage. Li'l Black Joe, from head to toe, yassuh,
yassuh, yassuh! Head to toe. The top part of my body
smelled different from the bottom part. My hair. My
arms. Between my fingers wasn't at all the same as between my toes. And between my legs. Daddy, somebody
in school said the funniest thing. She said her father told
her colored kids smell different from white kids. Is that
true?

26

Dear Mama and Daddy: I thought I'd like this place, but I had no idea summer camp would be such a nice place. Could I please stay two weeks instead of one? Your loving daughter, Dorothy Langan. They scraped the money together and I was allowed an extra week at that nice place. I hated that nice place but I had to stay longer so I could have a chance to get back at it. To save face. The Annual End-of-Summer-Camp-Follies was coming up and I was sure my dazzling tap dancing ability would rescue me from the disgrace of constantly sinking in the swim class. From the humiliation of showing up on the tennis court and being Dis-qualified because of the twenty-five-cent racket Mama bought me in the five and ten. Maybe it would even get me in with the most popular of the least popular kids. At the end of the extra week the show went on. After the performance a camp counselor took our picture. I still have it. In it all the campers are dressed alike. Adorable ballerinas in white bodices and net tutus. Pink satin toe shoes and tiaras. All but one. Way at the end of the line, almost out of the picture frame, a head shorter than the others, is a shoeshine "boy." In a turtleneck, baggy black pants, a striped suspender. Patent-leather tap shoes and a wool cap pulled way down over one eye. She is the one not looking at the camera.

27

The pilot's hat and goggles lay on a chair. My Cousin Brother Coley, the altar boy. Daddy said with rea-son-able certainty that some day his Nephew Brother Coley would join up with the Army Air Corps and become a crack pilot. He said he was really proud of that boy, Brother Coley. I'm gonna become a crack pilot, Daddy. No, you're not, Dorothy. Girls aren't allowed to serve in the Army Air Corps. The mailman arrived. Daddy left the lunchroom to meet him. Saying he was expecting something real important. I glared at those goggles and that hat. If there was one thing I didn't want to become, it was a crack pilot. I picked up that stupid hat. Boy, it was ugly. I put it on and climbed up on a stool. I looked at myself in the mirror. Through the letters advertising Moxie Soft Drink and past the picture of a pretty girl with long hair in a flowered bonnet saying, Umm-umm, Good! I put on the goggles. I wrapped a dish towel around my neck like a scarf. Cary Grant style. It didn't help. Well, I thought with rea-son-able certainty, I don't

care if I never serve in the Army Air Corps, and I don't
care if I never serve communion either. The door opened.
I didn't want Daddy to catch me in that stupid outfit. He
might get the wrong idea. Like that I liked them or something. I tried to yank them off and got tangled in the
straps. Dorothy! Look at this! I tried to turn my face
away. He was all flushed and waving a letter. Dorothy!
You've been accepted! For what, Daddy? For the Talented Child Contest in Perth Amboy. One goggle was on
my eye. One goggle was on my ear. The First Prize is a
Gold Bulova watch, twelve carats. With a stretch band
and a radium dial. Who the hell are you supposed to be in
that getup? Charlie Lindbergh? Who's Charlie Lindbergh? Who's Charlie Lindbergh! Only the biggest hero
America ever produced. He conquered the air. A-I-R,
Daddy? A-I-R, pal. He took the power of God Himself
and made it his very own. How? In an airplane. Airplanes
are okay. But tomorrow I'm gonna show you the greatest
way. The safest way to fly. How come it's the safest way,
Daddy? Because I say so. I smiled. He smiled. Are you
gonna win that Gold Bulova watch, pal? For me? Sure I
am, Daddy. I pulled off Brother Coley's stupid hat and
goggles and threw them on a chair. It floated through the
air. Silent. Like the biggest giant whale I ever saw in the
world. What is it, Daddy? A dirigible, pal. Lighter than
air. It's called the Hindenburg. And d'you know where
that Hindenburg is gonna land? It's gonna land right here
in our home state of New Jersey. Not in Woodbridge? No,
Dot, not in Woodbridge. I was glad of that. It was too
big. I reached out for my father's hand. And looked up. I
could see us. Him and me in that balloon. Soaring over
our house. On our way to Londontown. Paris. Spain.
Hollywood, California. And we wouldn't tell Mama. She
wouldn't even know we went off together. Till we got
back. And did God get mad at him for that, Daddy? For

what, pal? For going off with His A-I-R power. Oh, God's
got plenty more where that came from. Look at the size
of that balloon. I bet that balloon stole a lot of God's air,
too. Didn't it, Daddy? Well, sure it did. But God don't
mind. Believe me, if God minded, that thing wouldn't be
up there now. Sailing along. Safe as our house. Nothing
can ever happen to that balloon, pal. Trust me. I do,
Daddy. Okay, then. Let's go inside and turn on the radio.
And listen to the landing.

28

it's the safest way
i promise you
it's the only way to fly
my daddy said as he pointed up
at the great gray thing
in the sky
the great gray thing
in the sky
pal he said
(he called me pal)
we'll ride in that big balloon
some day we'll fly to londontown
we'll soar like
the silv'ry moon
we'll go to spain
and portugal
we'll fly to paris france
didya' know that ship
has a ballroom hall

where it's big enough
to dine and dance
with colored lights
and saxophones
oh yes dad
tell me yesyesyes
and didya' know
every night for dinner pal
the people have to wear
full dress?

wah wah wah
wah wah wah
wah wah wah
wah wah

i loved to hear him
talking talking
the safest way to fly
my daddy promised
and i trusted him
despite his
terrible eye
despite his
terrible eye
for i had not yet
felt his wrath
when i gazed at the gray balloon
and i dreamed of
going off with him
by the light of
the silv'ry moon
we ran inside the house
to hear on the
big brown radio
the actual real live

landing broadcast
the big ship was coming in slow
ladies and gentlemen
here she comes
the announcer gaily exclaims
she's gliding in like
a great gray bird
oh god
it's burst into flames. . . .

. . . my god
it's burst into flames
i can hear the
screaming screaming
everyone's doomed to
die
sweet jesus folks
it's a terrible sight
the announcer
starts to cry and i look
at my father's
eye
and
it suddenly seemed
too fearful
rimmed-red
as the edge of hell
and it fixed itself
upon me
and it burned
into every cell
it burned
into every cell

oh dad
the broken promises

hurt
more than broken bones
the people's screams
in the ballroom hall
drowned out
the saxophones

wah wah wah
wah wah wah
wah wah wah
wah wah

a great gray frog
now crouches
on the throne
of a former prince
and its endless
croaking croaking
has no power to convince
oh dad
you did me in that day
with the turn
of your terrible
eye
and
i cannot fly
and i will not fly
and i'm afraid to fly
ever since

wah wah
wah wah
wah wah
wah wah

29

DOROTHY LANGAN WINS FIRST PRIZE
AT PERTH AMBOY LAST SATURDAY.

WOODBRIDGE. Miss Dorothy Langan,
daughter of Mr. & Mrs. Michael
Langan, of Columbus Avenue, was
awarded first prize in the
Talented Child contest at the
Strand Theatre, Perth Amboy,
Saturday night. The girl was
awarded a gold wrist watch.
                    —*Perth Amboy Evening News*

But the Public was Fickle. To stay on top you had to keep
coming up with better Gimmicks. You had to be able to
do something nobody else thought of. And if they had,
they couldn't have done it anyway. There was one performer in our town who couldn't lose. The minute you
saw her come in the door you knew the best you could do
was second place. Every contest she entered she won. She

wasn't a particularly good tap-dancer and her singing was only so-so. But God-in-His-Infinite-Mercy had granted her an unbeatable Gimmick. She had only one arm. I envied that one-armed girl as much as cute ballerinas with ten-dollar tennis rackets and straight hair. Once, I dreamed of that little one-armed girl. I dreamed she met a one-armed boy. And together they made a person. Well, hell, pal, any damned kid in your class with two good arms can bend back, No Hands, and pick up a hankie with their teeth. But wait till you hear the sensational new Gimmick I thought up for you. Listening to the ball-game is when it came to me. Right in the middle of the third inning. With nobody on base. The commercial came on. And Pow! There it was. The greatest thing in the world. To replace the handkerchief trick. When you bend down backwards and you pick up this thing with your teeth. What thing, Daddy? The audience will stand up and cheer. What thing, Daddy? A double-edge razor blade, pal. Gillette. He wrote a letter to the company care of the radio station. He was willing he said to let them use his daughter's amazing trick. To be the basis for a big national publicity campaign. To include a picture of me doing my backbend and picking up one of their blades between my teeth. He informed them he was ready and available to meet with them. To come to terms as soon as possible. Since naturally there would be many other com-panies who would be interested. Sincerely, Michael J. Langan. Soon as I hear from them, pal, we're going off to Hollywood. The hell with New York City and Horn & Hardart's Kiddie Hours. He never heard from them. He issued his usual Boy-cott. And what with him shaving every other day. And what with me doing my amazing performance at numerous town functions, we figured the Gillette Razor Blade Company lost a couple of damned good customers.

30

Shirley Temple and Bill Bojangles Robinson did this really sensational routine. Bojangles was The Butler. Shirley was The Littlest Orphan. And they danced up and down the stairs of a beautiful mansion. On an old plantation. Somewhere in the Deep South. No sooner were we home from the movie when Daddy was down in the cellar. Every night he worked. On his latest invention for me. Incredible portable dancing steps. I loved to watch him work. Sawing and planing the wood. I especially liked his hands. I reached out. To feel one of the knots. At the same moment, he pursed his lips and blew. Sawdust flew into my eye. Everybody was up all night. With Mama treating me with boric-acid eye baths and with Daddy ranting and raving at Mama. It's em-bedded, that's what it is. That shit's buried in that eyeball forever. It's not embedded forever, Mike. What the hell are you doing with that rag? Cleaning the wound. You're making the wound worse. *You're* careless where you blow. *You're* too cheap to call a doctor. This kid could go blind in one eye while you sit swabbing with a lousy piece of rag, in order to save three lousy dollars for a house call. Why do you let her go down the cellar? Who can stop her? She's got your stubbornness. And your black temper. She has to bite the sheets to keep it in. Keep what in? Her black temper that she got from you. She's your kid, all right. Just *look* at her! *You* look at her! Neither one of them looked at me. I was forbidden to go near the *Incredible* portable steps again until they were finished and the unveiling took place. They were terrific. But the trouble was that they were so heavy no one could get them up the cellar stairs. Except with a dolly. Daddy said he'd just have to go along with me every time I performed. Mama suggested he put on black face and the two of us could dance a duet. Daddy scrutinized her. Are you being sarcastic? No, I'm not being sarcastic. Well, what made you think of that? Yellow shoes. Daddy's eyes softened. He smiled. Mama smiled. Remember, Mike, when we won the waltz contest together? Sure, Flo, I remember. He looked through the records. He found the right one and put it on the Victrola. Mama looked excited. The tune began. "Oh, Dem Golden Slippers." Her expression changed. I took Daddy's cue and danced up one spangled side of the steps and fell off the other. Daddy helped me up and asked me, was I hurt. I said no. And Mama left the room.

31

St. James' Players Give Fine Performance at Woodbridge

WOODBRIDGE. Approximately
1,000 persons crowded St. James'
auditorium to capacity last night
for the parish minstrel, "The
St. James' Jesters." The performance was brilliant and outstanding,
rivaling any similar affair held
here in years. The program was
in two parts, the first part being
"An Old Fashioned Schoolroom," with
Miss Susan Murphy as teacher. The
humorous antics of the pupils and
songs and dances were the highlights
of this scene. Miss Dorothy Langan
sang "Jeepers Creepers, Where'd You

Get Those Peepers?" She followed
this with a tap dance on ball-bearing
roller skates and concluded the
performance with a Buck and Wing
step and Trenches, garnering much
applause. . . .
                    —*Perth Amboy Evening News*

Daddy dug Trenches in the Big War. Daddy liked to go
around saying trenches held the piss of cowards and the
blood of heroes. Trenches also separated the good guys
from the bad. Daddy was on the side of the good guys. So
he won, but he got Gassed. Because of that experience
the Army Doctor told him he would be Ster-ile. Mama
sucked phlegm down from her sinuses into the back of
her throat. She spit into the kitchen sink and flushed it
down the drain with water from the cold-water faucet.
Might be Ster-ile, Mama corrected him. Mama always
corrected him on that word.

32

I'm sitting on the front porch, staring at my wart. Where do warts come from? They say if you touch a frog, a wart grows on the spot. Well, I have never swallowed an orange pit and I have never touched a frog. So how come I'm sitting here on the front porch with this thing growing on my knee? And Getting Worse? How come those things always turn up in my vicinity? You never saw any popular princesses in fairy tales with warts on their knees. Of course, they always wore long dresses. Very modest. Maybe their warts were only visible when you got real close. Or sneaked behind them, like the movie screen at the State Theater. Or maybe back in ancient times those royal ladies were able to touch enchanted frogs without contracting diseases and spoiling their reputation. Bile green frogs and royal princesses touching. Disgusting. I try to pick off the wart. When I pull it hurts. It's attached to me, or am I attached to it? Whichever it is, we're stuck with each other, and that's that.

33

Dorothy! Yes, Mama. Come into the kitchen a minute. What for? Don't ask what for when I call you! We got a swell surprise for you. Come in. But keep your eyes closed. No, not yet. I'll tell you when. Okaaaaay, open! *Boo!* A green head. No hair. No ears. And coiled around the skull, a snake. Coming from out of the mouth. No teeth. No tongue. Black metal-rimmed glass eyes. Popping. *Boo!* A dragon! A monster standing before me in our own kitchen! Not since the Convulsions have I screamed so loud. So loud *I* thought it was somebody else. Screaming. Somebody very close to the Purple Stage. Mama grabbed me. I wormed out of her grip. Have some water! I immediately stopped crying. Oh Dot, we didn't mean to scare you. It was only a joke. Daddy's joke. Not mine. It was Daddy all the time saying *Boo!* It wasn't Daddy saying *Boo!* Yesitwas. Take the mask off, Mike. No, don't take the mask off, Daddy. See. All it was was your own father in his old gas mask from The War. Isn't that a scream? Say yes. Yes. Then smile and show us you mean it.

34

Hey, where'd you get those flyspecks! I didn't even answer. If this ether smells bad, little girl, you just blow hard and it will all go away. He put the mask over my face. Bad! It smelled like garbage! I blew hard. It didn't go away. He lied to me. I was in the hands of a doctor I couldn't trust. I wasn't safe. I held my breath till I choked. I risked a couple of small gasps of air. I heard my breath come and go. Jerky. Like when you blow up a balloon. The balloon turned into a great gray frog. The more I gasped, the worse it smelled and the fatter the frog got till it took off and soared up into the sky over Maple Street and headed in the direction of London. I was going to lose it. Maybe I could've saved it. But the smell was too much. I blew and blew and blew. The frog exploded in the air and I exploded with it. My God, we've burst into flames. My God, we've burst into flames. Now I lay me down to sleep, I pray the Lord my soul to keep. If I should die before I wake. A wake is a funeral. A funeral is death. Death is a sleep. How can a sleep be A wake? Awake. Wake up, Dorothy. I woke up in the children's

ward of the St. Joseph's Ho-spit-al. I was spitting up
blood. Daddy woke up in the mental ward of the Soldiers'
Ho-spit-al in Paris, France. I wonder what he was spitting
up. Did somebody put the gas mask over his face and
then lie to him? If this smells bad you just blow it away.
Is that how he got Gassed? I took a deep breath. I began
to smell that terrible smell again. But I wasn't in the St.
Joseph's Ho-spit-al now. I was in our house. I was in our
kitchen. Scared to open my eyes again. And see that Bile
Green thing on daddy's face. Then I realized what that
smell was. Garbage. From Uncle Nick's truck. Uncle Nick
came running into the kitchen. I was over to the dump,
Mike, when I hit on this great idea. What the hell is that
on your head? My old gas mask, Nick. Oh. I was always
sorry, you know, Mickey. That they wouldn't take me on
account of my arm. I always though it was strange your
bad eyes didn't keep you out. What's the great idea
about, Nick? What? Oh, well, it's about Dot's dancing
and my accordion-playing. It's about how we're all gonna
go off to Hollywood and be in the movies.

35

GIVE MINSTREL
IN WOODBRIDGE
St. James' Players Score Another
Success, Capacity Audience.

WOODBRIDGE, Nov. 19. The St. James'
Players scored another success last
night when they presented a minstrel
show before a capacity house in the
St. James' auditorium. Under the
direction of John D. Campion, the
program opened with the entire en-
semble singing "Marching Along Together." A clever interpretation
of "Lazybones" was sung by Norman
Lewis following the opening number.
Margaret Dalton came next with
"Good Night Little Girl" and then
Leon Gerity with "That's How Rhythm
Was Born." Clair Bixel drew two

encores with his amusing imitation
of Bing Crosby as he sang "It's the
Talk of the Town." Marie Kowalzack
sang "The River's Takin' Care of Me"
and then Joseph O'Brien scored
another hit singing "Moonlight Down
in Lovers Lane."
Tom Ryan was next on the program
with a specialty tap dance number,
and Jack Keating drew many hearty
laughs as he sang "The Big Bad Wolf,"
assisted by his black-faced cohorts
on his second encore. Mrs. Genevieve
Neary was heard next singing the
popular number "Bless Your Heart."
Another of the "darkies" followed
Mrs. Neary and sang "Black-Eyed
Susan Brown" with all the accom-
panying motions and steps, much to
the delight of the audience. Ethel
Campion drew a good round of applause
when she sang "Just a Year Ago Tonight,"
and Jack Campion burlesqued his way
through "Are You Making Any Money?"
The last number was called "The
Domestic Farmers," a new trio about
town made up of Nick Langan, who
played the accordion; Tom Langan,
guitar; and George Cahill and his
harmonica. They played several cowboy
songs and then little Dorothy
Langan "stole the show" with her
remarkable tap dancing and singing . . .
—Perth Amboy Evening News

Daddy didn't play his clarinet well enough to be part of
Uncle Nick's new trio. But it was a hit. And Daddy was

sure we were on our way. And when we went off to
Hollywood, he was determined he wouldn't be left behind. So he appointed himself our official manager and
kept very busy with duties. For instance, the Changing of
the Name. For awhile the Name of the group was the
most important thing in Daddy's head. In Woodbridge
we were The Domestic Farmers. In Rahway we became
The Langan Family. George Cahill raised an objection to
that one. In Metuchen the billing was The Domestic
Mountaineers. In Carteret, The Domestic Hillbillies. And
in South Amboy we were the Hillbilly Trio, featuring
Dorothy Langan. Uncle Nick, who had a real good sense
of humor, made the suggestion to Daddy that he name us
Mike Langan's Daughter and Company.

36

Uncle Nick was what you'd call a bachelor till he was
thirty-five years old. Once, he was so rich he was Affected
By The Crash. He made a whole lot of money in some
kind of auto race-car track. Then he lost it all. I'm not
sure how. But it had something to do with gambling. He
was a real adventurer. And mysterious. If anybody could
get us to Hollywood, it was him. When I was walking
along with kids from our school and he drove past and
waved from the garbage truck, I waved right back.
Proud. Because I knew that under his trashman's coverall
there was a gambler, an auto racer, a miniature golfer,
and a hero. He had a withered arm and he played the accordion. He also did some of the masonry work on the
brook that divided our town. That brook was very important to us. A person's whole life was lived on one side or
the other. Us Irish Catholics had our neighborhood on the
right side. With our Church and our School. On the left
were the Rich Protestants with their Public School and
their tennis court. Above those two, the water sprang

from under the abandoned clay pits. Up there you had your Hungarians and your Polish. Hunkies and Poles we called them. Not to their faces. Those Hunkies and those Poles were an embarrassment to us Irish Catholics. All because Fate made one of those weird mistakes. Permitting those second-class foreigners to slip into our first-class religion. Fate probably felt dumb about the goof-up. But we were the ones who were stuck with them. Not Fate. Taking up space in Our Church. Using Our Religious Facilities. Praying in Our Pews. Not even in English. Smelling up the surroundings with their garlic breath from their pirogi. Once I was asked to tap dance at a benefit minstrel for the Protestant church. I was getting ready to go on when I heard the Inter-locutor telling a joke. About my song "Has Anybody Here Seen Kelly." About how you don't have to *see* an Irishman. You could *smell* an Irishman's beer breath a mile away. Everybody in the audience laughed. I didn't think it was so funny. I felt my face get hot. Protestants could always make Catholics feel embarrassed. Like we were beneath them or something. I didn't want to believe that. Us being born into the only True Faith. But whenever Uncle Nick drove past and waved at me from the garbage truck and I was walking along with Protestant kids I'd pretend I didn't see him. And I wouldn't wave back.

37

I'll never know how he managed to push those accordion buttons. What with a left arm that was withered, and Getting Worse. He had to work twice as hard as anybody to form the easiest chords. But he loved to play. He never acted like it wasn't getting any easier. And he always wore long-sleeved shirts. So nobody ever was subjected to the ugliness of the Deformity. But once in Lake Hopatcong, when he was changing in the bath house, Mama came in unexpectedly. Without knocking. And she got a glimpse of the ugliness of the Deformity. No bigger than a baby's wrist, she said. Nobody knows how it happened. Sometime back before he was five that left arm just stopped growing and never did grow again. The rest of his arm appeared normal in every way, shape, and form. Just like Daddy's or Mama's or mine. How could a person have a grown-up's hand and wrist and a little baby's arm? What made something stop growing and never grow again? Stunted. Infant-ile Pa-ralysis. Godblessthemark. I wondered if he was born right-handed. I never asked. I thought I knew the answer. Right is the angel's side. Left is the you-know-what's. Mother's milk itself actually turned black as Bosco in the breast if the baby drank from the evil side. So it was possible that an upper arm could get Pa-ralyzed if God-in-His-Infinite-Wisdom caught that little Infant sucking on the Devil's Thumb.

38

the left hand is
we always say
the demon devil's side
the left hand does
the dirty work
the shameful things
you hide
judas kissed the left cheek of christ
it's satan's special mark
there were no left-footed animals
allowed on noah's ark
left-handed people are impure
they go against the grain
left-handed children
play with themselves
and drive themselves insane
. . . .

my right hand fills the china teacups
and needlepoints with old maid aunts

my right hand clings to rosary beads
and waters dying plants
but it's never painted a picture
nor run for president
my left hand
might have done these things
if its roots
had not been bent
a sculptor
a poet
it might have been
instead of a useless thing
to decorate with bangles and bracelets
and my mother's wedding ring

something
it might have accomplished
or nothing
now i'll never know
oh
my lost
my left
my natural hand
my god
i miss you so

39

Cuuup! Does Dorothy want the cup? Okay, she can have it. Not with that hand! No? Okay, then you can't have the cup at all. Mama will keep the cup for herself. Umm, it tastes good. Bosco. But Dorothy can't have any. Bosss-co! Want! Where did the cup go? Is Mama hiding the cup behind the chair? Point to the cup. With the other hand, or Mama won't sit beside Dorothy any more. Mama will go away. Here she goes. Good girl, now baby can have the Bosco. No, don't take, Mama will give. Same hand. Same! Take the cup with the right. Riiight. Right, Right! What a good baby she is. Now drink all the Bosco and you'll get to see little Miss Muffet sitting at the bottom of the cup eating her curds and whey when along came a spider who sat down beside her and frightened Miss Muffet away. Right. Riiight. Right. Riiight.

40

In our front yard was a big tree. In the wintertime, if I sat on the stoop and stared long enough, the tree would seem to be growing upside down, with the head stuck in the ground and the roots em-bedded in space. Space was scary. It wasn't real. My house was real. Space was Holy Ghosts and no-face Demons and no-name Angels. Space was filled with mysterious and terrifying places. Heaven. Hell. Eternity. Limbo. Purgatory. Oh, God. I saw the initials. I always saw the initials in words. I didn't want to see the initials. But there they were. H-E-L-P. I didn't want to see H-E-L-P. I didn't want to know that. I didn't want to be able to figure things out. Let somebody else figure out that those words spelled H-E-L-P. Let them put it in the Catechism where it belonged under H. It wasn't my place to make up new Gimmicks, only to know what I'd been taught and told. Don't do as I do, do as I say. Because I say so. What do you know, you're only a child. An orange tree will grow in your stomach if you swallow the pits. The angel's side is the right. A dirigible is the safest way to fly. But it isn't. Okay. Okay. Then the left arm is not withered and Getting Worse. But it is. The tree is always right side up. But it isn't. There is no H-E-L-P. No heaven, hell, eternity, limbo, purgatory. But there is. There is no Hollywood. But I saw a picture of it in a magazine. We will get there someday. Soon. Why? Because I say so. Unless I become a nun.

41

when she made her first communion
esther made the perfect union
in her dress of white and wispy veil
esther's parents said to please us
you got to go and marry jesus
and her father took her to the altar rail

when she made her first communion
esther made the perfect union
and that night she thought of him in bed
she decided if he sees us
we ought to get a look at jesus
and she began to see the one she wed

i began to see little jesus
he was sitting on my bed
that's what esther told her mother
and to which her mother said
you're an evil child to tease us
glory be i hope to jesus

that your father never hears this
he would wash your mouth with soap

when she made her first communion
esther made the perfect union
but she never saw his face again
yeah, her mother said, don't tease us
so instead of seeing jesus
she began to see a lot of other men

what she saw was quite a collection
older men and young ones too
cousins friends and even a brother
one at a time or quite a few
she began to see a gay uncle
who resembled billy graham
she began to see perfect strangers
she didn't even know by name

when she made her first communion
esther made the perfect union
but she never saw his face again
yeah, her mother said, don't tease us
so instead of seeing jesus
she began to see a lot of other men
but she never told her mother again
no she never told her mother again

42

Mama pinned the blue sateen rosettes to the white Chantilly lace Communion Veil. I was crazy with excitement. But careful not to show it and make waves. Mama put the Veil on my head. She looked at my reflection in the Bevelled-edge dining room mirror. Well, you're not *exactly* pretty. But in that Veil and all, you know what they say. All brides are beautiful. Bride of Jesus? Gift of God? I turned around. Mama was staring past my shoulder. I never had a Veil. Your father and me, we were married so *fast*. She yanked the Veil off my head. She pulled my hair. Ouch. Oh, Dot, I didn't mean to. I didn't care. I hadn't seen an outfit so important-looking since Brother Coley's pilot hat and goggles. I liked Brother Coley a whole lot. Actually, I didn't like him at all. Catholics are forbidden to have a crush on cousins and other blood relations. The next time I ran into Brother Coley I would be sure to act very stand-offish. That way God would see that I had no Impure Thoughts regarding a blood relation. Mama, how do you make a baby? Shit! The thread broke, the bobbin got tangled. Mama? Mama was very busy. She worked the thread back and forth till she freed it. She wet the tip with her lips and tried to thread the needle. Mama? She missed the hole several times before she was able to pull the thread out the other side. She tucked it under the foot and shoved the ribbon loops under the needle. I never saw her so occupied. Mama, how? Shit! She was sewing her finger. Why was she acting that way? Taking such chances. She knew how stubborn the Singer Sewing Machine was. You can't rush it. You have to calm down and take it step by step or the Singer Sewing Machine will break down before your very eyes. She herself told me that. But there she was with her pierced finger. She spit on it and put it in her mouth. She sucked. Lucky it was her right finger. Mama? She slammed her fist down on the Veil. Oh, all right! You know that thing a man has? What thing? That, you know, *thing*. She crooked her finger at me. Broken nail. Half-moon. Deep ridges. Rough cuticle. Point bent backwards. Blob of Snow White spit. And behind the spit a small bubble of blood. Rose Red's teardrop. Well, the man, he takes that thing that he has and he sticks it in the lady and that's how babies are made. You understand? No. But I was too embarrassed to ask any questions. Ever again. She must've got the image across to me, though. Because when I got bigger and I finally figured out how to touch myself Down There, the thing I used to do it with was a bottle of nail polish. I can't think of the shade. But the brand, I remember, was Cutex.

43

Communion was Sunday. Bright stained glass. Happiness, He is Risen this Glorious Morn and the singing of Choirs. Confession was Saturday. Dark drapes. Penance, guilt, and the telling of Sins. First Communion was Saints and New White Shoes. First Confession was Satan and Stations of the Cross. Confession was horrible but without it there couldn't be any wonderful Communion and vice versa. How come? Did that mean without bad there couldn't be any good? It couldn't mean that. I know it couldn't. What do you know? You're only a child.

44

The visiting nurse came to examine us. And I showed all the Symptoms. Diphtheria. Everybody got all excited. Like I was really important. Then everybody backed away from me. Like I was this evil, unhealthy person. All of a sudden, they rushed me out. Home from school. For what they called the Protection of the kids. But what about the Protection of me? I was I-solated. But the Symptoms had been sent home with me. They were right there in the room. In my bed. In my body. I felt like two people. Here was the healthy me. Under my skin and under the covers. Lying with the unhealthy me. I didn't want to be there. In that room. Alone. With some kind of fight going on inside me. I wanted to be back in school with the other kids. Doing arithmetic and eating lettuce sandwiches for lunch. I prayed, begged, and made bargains with God-in-His-Infinite-Generosity to save me from my bad side. And it worked. Because one day the Doctor informed Mama that the Symptoms had all disappeared. But where did they go? I peered around the dark room. I peeked under the bed. I felt under the pillow. Mama raised the shade. The sun streamed in. There were no more shadows. There were no more Symptoms hiding in the shadows. There was no more evil, unhealthy me.

45

Mama, Mama! I'm tainted! You're not tainted, stop crying. I am tainted! Who says? The kids in school. Once you get Diphtheria, they said it never leaves you. They said you carry it around inside you forever. That's not Diphtheria, that's Typhoid Fever. Typhoid Fever never leaves you. But Mama, how come when Ruthie Cahill broke her leg all the kids stood around and stood around looking at her cast? And how come everybody thinks Pat Lane's cleft palate is so terrific? Why is it when other kids get something wrong with them they just get more popular and dogs never run after them. There's a reason dogs run after you, Dot. But, down at the State Theater there's only the good movie guys and the bad movie guys, period. How come I feel good and very popular *inside*? But *outside* I'm unpopular and tainted? I get so mixed up. You want to know why you get mixed up, Dorothy? I'll tell you exactly why you get mixed up. You were born under a Bad Sign. Bad Sign? You mean, The Veil? Yes. The Veil and The Time. Your birth certificate states that you were born at Twelve-O-Five. To avoid future confusion. Actually, you arrived at the stroke of Midnight. Babies born at that moment will never be sure who they are. The superstition is, they go through life not knowing whether they want to go back to the day before Midnight, or go ahead to the day after. They're forever divided. The Midnight Baby is called Twice Born. And that's what you are, Dot. Twice Born.

46

Something shifted. Heavy, behind the dark screen. Then it mumbled. I didn't understand. I leaned in. It had Terrible Breath. I backed away. But it moved closer. I was cornered. It mumbled again and gestured. I couldn't figure out anything it was saying. Some foreign language. Have I gotten stuck with some Polish priest? Then I made out a couple of words. Latin. Those I understood. I didn't really understand. But I knew that anything in Latin was real religious and very holy. Latin words were words I could trust. They were safe. So was I. All right. In the Name of the Father. And of the Son. And of the Holy Ghost, Amen. This is my first Confession, Father. I accuse myself of. I was shaking, afraid all the nuns' hard work might not pay off. For months they'd been drumming Sins and the Recognizing of Same into our noggins. And we had become real experts on being ever on Guard against ourselves. The bigger the Sin we caught ourselves at, the prouder we were. Venial Sins being okay but Mortal Sins being everybody's Big Goal. But, for me, Filling the Quota was a problem. I had spent a lot of time worrying about it. What if I hadn't come up with a big enough list of sins? Maybe I could invent some. Not actual outright *lies*, mind you. That would be dis-honest. The trick would be to take something that looked innocent enough. And twist it until it was possible to Interpret Same as Con-stituting a Mortal Sin. With practice maybe I could get good at it. After awhile, I'd be able to take the most honest word or deed and, if I picked at it long enough, I'd be able to come up with something of value. Implied Guilt. Evil Intention. Then there was always Impure Thoughts. That was a handy category. I could actually have a reserve stock of those. So I could never be caught short. Because the most important thing in the world was to Impress the Priest. I would go to any lengths not to let him down. And the best way not to let him down was to come in Prepared. With a Full Quota. That was called Pleasing the Priest. What did I catch you doing behind the Campions' garage with Billy Herron? He asked me to show him what I had, Mama. And did you? Yes. Did he show you what he had? Yes, he showed me. And are you sorry you did that? No. What'd you say? No, Mama. Come back here! Hand me that hairbrush! I'll fix you so you'll *never* say no to me again as long as you live! Pull up your dress, pull down your pants, bend over! Showing mine to Billy Herron. Implied Guilt. Letting Billy Herron show me his. Evil Intention. Saying No to my mother. Mortal Sin. Then, later, *thinking* about showing and looking with Billy Herron. Impure Thought. A good big list. I rattled them off. The head nodded. I was given penance and absolution. I left the confessional with a light heart. I had passed the test. I qualified as a Sinner.

47

Priests and boys were permitted behind the Communion Rail at any time. Nuns were permitted behind the Communion Rail under certain circumstances. To change dead flowers, to replace burned-out candles, to change the soiled altar cloth, and to scrub the floors. Nuns were never allowed behind the Communion Rail during the ceremonies except for Mary's Crowning. Girls who were not nuns or crowners were not allowed behind the Communion Rail at any time. Ever. Period.

48

I'm kneeling at the railing in my white dress and Chantilly lace Veil with the bunched-up blue rosettes. A terrific virginal effect except for the slight stain from Mama's finger prick. I wish I was popular. I look past the crucifix to her statue. The Virgin Mary. Standing on top of the world, keeping Satan in check with her dainty foot. There's no getting around it. She's popular. And pretty. In every way, shape, and form. Except for her bare foot, she's completely dressed. Modest. Covered. Not like her only Son, Jesus. I look back at the crucifix. Her only Son, Jesus, is hanging from the cross in nothing but His loin cloth. Covering His Loins. The inside of His thighs. Between His legs. Between Jesus' legs? Boy, I certainly didn't want to think about that. Talk about an Impure Thought of gigantic proportions. But I could never in a million years bring myself to confess that one no matter how much it might Please the Priest. He's up to the girl next to me. I can't stand the beauty of it. My cousin, Brother Coley, is the server. I wish he'd come and take his rotten hat and goggles. For all I cared, he could wear them behind the Communion Rail. The girl next to me snaps open her mouth to Receive. The girl next to me's jaw cracks. Does it taste sweet? Bitter? Does it taste? My eyes snap over at Jesus' loins. Dear God, why can't I take my eyes off Jesus' loins? If only the priest would hurry. Oh, God, he's in front of me. Blocking out the sight of the Holy Thighs. What was I supposed to do? Oh, yes. I stick out my tongue. I can't make it stop wiggling. I'm so embarrassed. His fingertip is wet. The girl next to me's spit. Disgusting. I clamp my eyes shut. He enters my mouth. My tongue is barely skimmed and he's gone. Already on to the next little girl. It's over already. But that's all right. Inside he has left the Body of Jesus. Round and soft and no taste. Loins. I hurry to get up. My knees are shaking. Lean Loins. I run away back down the aisle. Lean Loin Lamb. That's what Mama sends me for at the butcher's. Lean Loin Lamb Chops. That's what's on my mind. Not the Other. See how it works? With a little effort the most Impure Thought can be turned into the most Pure Thought. I am not a bad girl. I have not been thinking of Jesus' loins. I have been thinking of meat. I hate meat. Hate is a bad word. Here I am, with His blessed Body still fresh in my mouth and I've already Sinned. Oh God-with-Your-Infinite-All-Seeing-Eye, please overlook this miserable creature with all her hate, meat, loins, and other Impure Thoughts. Please do not punish her by doing something like letting the Host fall out of her mouth in front of the entire congregation. Please, please, please. It's stuck to the roof of my mouth. I press It with my tongue. I can't get It unstuck. I try to pull at It with the tip of my tongue but am afraid I might bruise It with my teeth or otherwise bite on It. Under no circumstances are we to chew on the Holy Body. I long to stick my finger into my mouth and pry It loose with my nail. But

the nuns had warned us. Girls were forbidden to lay a
hand on the Holy Body. Period. If the absolute worst ca-
tastrophe happened and you dropped It and you are a girl,
you are to step back. Then you are to signal the nearest
nun who in turn will summon an altar boy, who will no-
tify a priest who will come out from behind the altar rail
and with Consecrated Hands he will retrieve the Holy
Presence from the floor. My mouth is shut so tight that
my jaws are beginning to ache. What if I can't hold out
until I find my pew? What if I can't find my pew? Where
do I belong? I've lost my way. There's a Station of the
Cross. Veronica. My pew is near that Station. Veronica is
wiping the bloody brow of Jesus with her Veil. Veronica
was a girl. How come in those days girls were allowed to
lay their hands on the Holy Body? I wondered if we committed some terrible sin in the meantime and became
unclean. Veronica's Veil. Veil. Gauze. Loin Cloth. Loins.
Lean Loins. Lean Loin Lamb. Jesus' loins. I'm going to
kill myself. There's a prayer book. My initials are stamped
in the right-hand corner. D. V. L. Initials. I'm in trouble.
Add an E and an I. Don't think. And D. V. L. spells
DEVIL. Stop it, Dorothy! Dark Versus Light. Deity
Versus Lucifer. Dorothy Views Loins. Disgusting Sinner.
I fall to my knees in my pew. I try to pray the Impure
Thoughts out of my miserable head. But all-night fasting
has left me light-headed and I'm thirsty. At the back of
my dry throat the Heavenly Host is bunched up as badly
as my blue rosettes. I try to work up some spit to swallow.
I remember my deathly fear of choking. How am I going
to get rid of this pasty lump? Forgive me, Father. I gulp.
The air goes down but Jesus stays up. Oh, God, are You
actually going to let me strangle to death on Your only
living Son in Whom You are well pleased? It's impossible,
but I've eaten enough Wonder Bread in my life to know
that bread does not melt. So I may have to sit here with

His pasty remains stuck in my throat forever. Well, for some reason, the prospect of living with Jesus Christ our Lord inside me throughout eternity has an odd effect on me. My spit starts building up. I think I'm achieving sainthood. My mouth actually waters. The Holy Body breaks up into little pieces. He is in the back of my throat. I panic. But finally He goes down. I have swallowed the Host. His Most High and Holy Body. All. All but His Blood. Only the Man Priest Boy may taste His Holy Blood. The Holy Blood may never be tasted by the female nun woman girl. Period. But all the *rest* of Him is in my stomach. Head, Body, Arms, Legs, and Loins.

49

That winter Uncle Nick's Deformity took a Turn for the Worse. The trio broke up and I was back on my own. Daddy took to writing letters again. To programs on the order of "Grand Ole Opry." He even had me write a personal fan letter to one of the Opry's leading lady singers. Neither one of us ever heard. The lady didn't even send the autographed picture I requested. Daddy's face got beet red every time he talked about it. Which was almost always. Why should those big people answer your letters, Mike? Because I say so, Flo! But they're so busy and they don't know if Dot's as good as you say. Are you callin' me a liar, Flo? No, Mike, it's just that, well, the Shirley Temple of Woodbridge could be an exaggeration. Are you calling me a liar, Flo? The sun don't rise and set in her! It does if I say it does! Isn't that reason enough? If that ain't reason enough, I want to know now, Flo! It's reason enough, Mike. It's reason enough.

50

When Daddy beat up Mama and pushed her down the flight of stairs, she ran out of the furnished apartment and went wandering around. Blindly. Until all hours of the night. Not noticing that it happened to be pouring rain and not caring that she was getting soaked to the skin. Actually, she told me she was hoping she'd get Pneumonia. Then we'd both die and he'd be sorry for the rest of his life for the way he treated her and for saying that the child she was carrying in her stomach wasn't his. It was just before dawn when she realized she was on the far side of the brook. She swears she doesn't remembering crossing the bridge. But there she was in foreign territory. She heard a growl. She turned around. Something moved in the shadows. A big Protestant Police dog sprang from the bushes. Looking like it was having a fit. Teeth like fangs. Eyes like the Devil's. It jumped right for her stomach. She was nearly knocked down by the weight of me and the beast. She jumped back. It only nipped her right hand. But God knows what might have happened if she hadn't screamed. The dog reared back and cocked its head like it was surprised. Then it ran off into the night as quick as it came. Now this may seem very strange, but Mama swears to this day that it was as if that big police dog knew I was inside her. She likes to think that I felt that beast go for me. But I like to think that's what she got for going into the Protestant section. She also likes to think that's why dogs run after me. Because I'm afraid. When you're afraid, Dorothy, dogs smell it. Smell what, Mama? Smell *it*.

51

Where's Daddy's bird dog, Mama? He snapped at your father. Drew blood. Your father said, I'll show you, you bastard, and he beat him across the back. With his belt? Oh, Mama, not with the chain. Listen, Dot, the dog's better off run away. I wish Daddy was—. It's not your father's fault. When the Devil's in him, he's not responsible. Believe me, Dot, I know. He could kill you as easy as look at you. What does that word mean? What word? Bastard. Don't ever let me hear you say that word again. That's a dirty, filthy word. What does that word mean? It means a dog. With no father? What did you say? I didn't say anything.

52

Is he starting that shit again, Florence? No, Rose, no.
Then why the hell were you crying when I came in? Oh,
Rose, it's so embarrassing. I can't tell you what he did.
Tell me, Florence. He went over to the Rectory and he
got down on his knees in front of the priest. In the Rectory! Why the hell'd he do that? He ain't sorry at this late
date, is he? For the way he treated you when Dot, here,
was born? No, Rose. I asked him was that it. What'd he
say? He just gave me his usual answer. Well, what goes
on behind your own walls is your own beeswax. But if he's
gonna start making a god-damned fool of himself in the
Rectory, I say it's time to straighten him out. No, Rose, let
Nick do it. He respects his brother. Let Nick. Maybe they
could even play a few tunes together. Florence, did it
ever strike you as funny? How all the Langan boys played
instruments? After our pa's musical prowess? And none of
the girls? Over ten kids in the family and not one damned
girl ever touched an instrument. Mike hasn't touched his
clarinet in months, Rose. I hid his gun. You hid his gun?

Why? Did that bastard have the gall to threaten you? No, it's just that, well, last night, he had a dream about the war. Well, if he starts up, Florence, you just let me know. Maybe I ain't able to carry a tune in a bucket. But I sure am able to give him a good tongue-lashing. Put him in his place, y'understand? I understand. He hasn't had a dream about the war in a long time.

53

It was such a cute little park. Lots of pointy grass. Twisting trees. Clumps of pansies. Grinning between the purple mossy roots. The crooked paths were lined with poppies, red as the stripes on the flags we were carrying. The gates were gray. Standing straight as pitchforks. When we went through, the guard had given us each a little gilt-tipped flag and a pass. I was so excited. Mama told me to simmer down. But I knew. It was a picnic. We took the widest path. It led us up to the edge of a hill. Over the rim was a deep pit. In the middle of the pit was a beautiful big building. Veterans Ho-spit-al. What does that mean, Mama? It means I have to go in without you. How come? Other kids are going in. Not into Daddy's ward. Kids aren't allowed in Daddy's ward. Aunt Mamie will wait outside with you and keep you company while Uncle Harry goes in with me. I looked at my flag. When I looked back she and Uncle Harry were gone. Aunt Mamie was rummaging through her purse. I got Dentyne, Sen-Sen, Life-Savers, and I got Tums. What'll you have?

Life-Saver, please. I put it in my mouth. Wintergreen.
The first one I ever tasted. What a name. Wintergreen.
Winterbrown, maybe. Or Winterblack. Summergreen, of
course. But Winter-green? Never. Right then, I got so
mad at the makers of Life-Savers. Why was Hollywood,
where it was so hot you could go swimming in December,
named after a winter flower? Why were grown-ups, who
were in charge of such stuff, always naming things
wrong? I mean, if a pit is something inside an orange or
an apple, why is it also a hole in the ground? I didn't
know and I didn't care. Not only that, I decided those
grounds weren't all that great. And as for the Veterans
building, it was just plain ugly. The shape was ugly. The
doors were ugly, and the windows were the most ugly,
with those metal fences in front of them like the gorilla
cages in the zoo. You finished your Life-Saver, Dorothy?
No, I wanted to say, I am not finished my Life-Saver! I
will probably never finish my Life-Saver as long as I live!
I wanted to yell. But I couldn't speak up. Let me see your
tongue, Dorothy. If it's all gone I'll give you another one.
I don't want another one, thank you. Why're you gasp-
ing? Didn't you like it? Yes, Aunt Mamie. If you didn't
like it, spit it out in my hand. I can't spit it out, Aunt
Mamie. And I'll give you a Tum, instead. It's stuck in my
throat, Aunt Mamie. Oh, well, in a little while it'll melt
and I promise you won't feel a thing. Look, Dorothy,
surprise! Mama was coming out of the building. Holding
a wadded hankie up to her eyes. Run, Dorothy! Go meet
your mother and your Uncle Harry! I didn't move. Scared
that if I budged, the Life-Saver would drop from my
throat, into my windpipe, get em-bedded in my lungs, cut
off my air supply and choke me to death. Yoo-hoo, wave,
Dorothy! Wave to your father like a good girl! Where?
Up there! I looked up. He was standing on the balcony.
One hand was hanging on to the ugly metal fence. Gray

flannel bathrobe. No cord. Pajamas in the daytime. He was waving with the hand that wasn't holding on. I wasn't waving back. An obedient child doesn't make waves. Why should she? Mama could go in to see him. Other relatives like uncles that weren't as close could go in to see him. But the obedient child had to stay outside like a dummy. He didn't even have on his glasses. His bare eyes and open robe made me feel embarrassed. My throat got tighter. The Life-Saver shifted. The pain of the shift brought tears to my eyes. I struggled to catch my breath. Everybody was looking at me. Somebody patted me on the head. There, there. They kept looking from me up to Daddy and back to me again. Shaking their heads. Like they felt bad. I don't know who they were doing their headshaking for. I was okay. I just kept swallowing until the Life-Saver melted away. And just like Aunt Mamie promised, I didn't feel a thing. I wasn't going to choke to death after all. Smile, Dorothy! I didn't smile. Then I saw he was wearing paper slippers. I smiled. He smiled. He turned and went back inside. I suddenly got sad that the Life-Saver was melted. He's gone, Mamie. No, Floss, I think I just caught a glimpse of him behind the curtain. Wave, Dorothy! In case he can still see you! I didn't wave.

54

the princess
let her hair
hang down
for the young
adoring knave
he climbed halfway
when he heard her say
i swoon
to be your slave
when his chin appeared
on the window ledge
the princess' face
turned grave
my passion's ceased
be gone
you beast
till you've
switched to
Burma Shave

55

Daddy had a license. When he was younger he drove a truck. Every three years since then he went down to the license bureau and renewed it so he wouldn't have to take an eye test and fail. His eyes were that bad. These glasses are real expensive, Mickey, you be careful or I'll know the reason why, you hear? He was in the second grade when his father bought him that first pair of glasses. The next day a kid in the schoolyard jumped on his back and knocked the glasses to the ground. The kid stepped on them and ran away. Where are your glasses, Mickey? They broke, Pa. You broke them! No, somebody else broke them. You're a liar! He beat him across the back with his belt. He beat him till he fell to the floor. Then he beat him till he couldn't get up from the floor. When his father stormed out of the kitchen, Daddy swore to the linoleum that he'd never wear another pair of glasses. Not until he could pay for them. Out of his own pocket. By the time he was ten years old his eyes were so strained he couldn't read the print in his school books. Or in his music books. His am-bition was to be a clarinet player. But as his eyes got weaker, his mind got slower. His marks failed. In the sixth grade he quit. In no time at all he got a job in the clay pits. He finally bought and paid for his own silver-rimmed glasses. Out of his own pocket. He didn't have much use for them by then. Him being a laborer digging ditches. He thought about maybe taking some music lessons but his natural-born ability was gone. It was too late. He hated not being on time for anything. After he dressed to go somewhere he always sat with his pocket watch placed on the table where he could keep an eye on it. Tick. Tick. But no matter how late it was, he never left the house without checking his wallet to be sure he had his driver's license. He always carried it with him. Up-to-date and promptly renewed. I never understood why he needed that license. Since we never owned a car.

56

I had no inkling, Mamie. No inkling at all there was anything wrong. Oh, he mentioned getting Gassed, and yes, there were some references to Shell-Shock. Don't wave the flag out the window, Dorothy. It's liable to break. But he had all his arms and his fingers and his legs, not to mention his eyes. So why would I think there would be anything, you know, wrong with him? Ma never wanted you to marry him, Flossie. I know. She locked me in a closet, remember, Mamie? If Pop hadn't climbed in through the trap door and helped me escape, I'd have married somebody else. Was there somebody else, Floss? No, Harry, that was just a figure of speech. Who married you, Floss? The Army Chaplain. Then they led Mike away. Under Armed Guard. So he wouldn't try to desert his country and go off with his bride. Were there a lot of deserters, Floss? None that I saw, Harry. The day was so romantic. With the band playing. The flags flying. The troop ship sailing away. And me waving right up to the last. When it all just disappeared into the horizon. Then I went back. Past the coal barges. Back to Ma's house. I had to keep my job as a telephone operator during the day. But at night I did my bit. I rolled bandages. I know, Flossie. Yes, but what you didn't know was that the more bandages I rolled, the more I started to worry. Would one of those bandages be used on him? Would he be wounded? Would he be killed? Would I be a widow before I was ever a wife? I nearly went crazy. But I never let on, did I? No, Flossie, but you didn't speak to Ma for months. Why should I? The way she treated me. But then, everything was all right. When I saw how Mike came back from overseas. Didn't he come back by troopship, Floss? I mean, he came back whole. With all his vital parts. I was so relieved. And so happy to leave Ma's house and settle down with him in our own apartment. Was that the two-room apartment, Floss? Yes, Harry, and it wasn't a week before I realized. Ma had been right. After he had his first nightmare.

57

Dirty low fuckin' bastard! You ain't gettin' me! I'll kill you first! Mike! Mike! It's me, Florence! Huh? What? Who is it? My throat, Mike! Mygod! You were trying to strangle me! Jesus, Flo, I'm sorry, he said. I put on the light. Don't go away, Flo, he said. Please. I got to talk to somebody. It was so terrible. So I stayed there and let him talk. Mother of God, Mamie, you can't imagine what he told me. Such awful a-trocities. You don't know how it felt to lay there in those trenches. Waiting in the pitch dark for the enemy to sneak up on you. You didn't dare sleep. Who knew when it might happen? But when your eyes burned so bad you couldn't keep them open any more, you said the hell with it. And you shut them tight. But even if the bay-onets didn't get you and the shells missed you, you were still prey to the Invisible Monster. Creeping. Odor-less. Dorothy, will you stop crowding me! Where was I? The Invisible Monster, Mama. Oh, thanks, Dot, I didn't know you were listening. Anyway, the Invisible Monster, as they called it, killed untold numbers of our brave boys at the front while they slept like innocent babes. But now here's the kicker—they were regarded as the more fortunate ones. The brave boys that lived and thought they'd escaped didn't find out till later that the Invisible Monster had crawled into their very organs. Contaminating some of their lungs. Tainting some of their blood cells. And leaving some of them Sterile. Sterile, Mike? I said. Sterile. What does that mean? You know what that means, Flo, he said. No, Mike, I said. I don't know what it means. It means that you're not able to, you know, have children. My God, I said. Don't cry, Flo, he said. I'm beggin' you. Please. Don't cry.

58

Ever since then I've slept light, believe me, Harry. Eventually, he stopped having the nightmares. Most of the time, he didn't even dream. Just lay there all night without moving a single muscle. But I was on guard, Harry. I was on guard and sure enough, I was right. There he is in the Veterans' Ho-spit-al as living proof of my suspicions. I read this story once about Typhoid Mary. Did you ever read that story about her, Harry? She seemed not to have the Fever. But she had all the Symptoms. Hiding inside of her. Where were the Symptoms hiding, Mama? Not now, Dorothy. I'm talking to your Uncle Harry and your Aunt Mamie. Those Symptoms just lay there. Sleeping like a dragon. Sleeping and growing stronger. Sleeping and biding their time till they could jump out and attack the closest person to Typhoid Mary. Typhoid Mary looked perfectly healthy. But she was A Carrier.

59

Are you absolutely sure, Mike? Well, no, not absolutely. What do you mean not absolutely? Did he say you were or did he say you weren't? He didn't say either. Well, what exactly did he say? He said it was possible. Possible? Is that the actual word the doctor used? Not the actual word. Might was the actual word. *Might what? Might be!* He said I *might be* Sterile. Catholics are *Forbidden* to use Con-tra-cep-tives. Any Catholic who confesses to using those is in big trouble. Stop immediately, if not sooner. If you continue using those after confessing same, you are in for the worst of all possible rejections. Worse than Mortal Sin. Worse than Limbo. Worse than Purgatory. But it was you, Mike. You were the one who took Precautions. I never used anything. *You* committed the sin. *My* conscience is clear. *My* soul is safe.

60

The Doctor was telling me such crazy stuff in the Ho-
spit-al. About how some men feel guilty. Especially Catholic men. About having, you know, sexual relations. That
Doctor said a Catholic man can actually make himself believe he isn't having anything to do with his own wife. Until she gets pregnant. Then he can't lie to himself any more.
Turn the radio up, Harry. I want to ask you something,
Mamie. And little pitchers have big ears. Would Harry
mind, you know, *using* something, Mamie? You kidding,
Flossie? Harry's a lukewarm Catholic at best. Once I
made divinity fudge and he ate a piece before communion. Broke his fast and still received. I told it the next
week in confession. The next week? Weren't you afraid of
the Wrath of God, Harry? No, Floss. It's my belief you
got to use your religion. You can't let it use you. We were
married so many years, Mike and me, before we had
Dorothy. She was an accident. On his part, not mine.
Maybe he really thought that Doctor in Paris, France,
was right. And he stopped using. But that Doctor in Paris,

France, was wrong. Well, he made me get down on my knees and swear to him. How can I be sure, he said. Go and get a test, I said. If I do, he said, and it's negative, Flo, I'll kick you out on your ass. But he wouldn't get a test. Oh no. I guess he was more afraid of his religion. I mean, if he got that test and it was positive, the Holy Mother Church would kick him out on his ass. *Ex-com-mun-ica-tion!* Ex-com-mun-ica-tion, capital E-x-c-o-m-m-u-n-i—. You don't have to spell it, Dorothy. Let her spell it if she wants to, Floss. Spell, Dot! Spell and I'll give you another Life-Saver. No, thanks, Aunt Mamie. See, she doesn't want to spell. She just wants to get our attention. To let us know she's here. We know you're here, Dot. Just settle down. We know you're here.

61

we never stop to wonder
till a person's gone
we never yearn to know him
till he's travelled on
when someone is around us
we never stop to ask
hey, what's behind your mirror
hey, who's beneath your mask
we never stop to wonder
till a person's gone
we never yearn to know him
till he's packed
and travelled on
. . . .
sweet beautiful jesus
on a painted cross
polystyrene body
with a superficial gloss
hey, were you

jealous of your father?
were you short
when you were fully grown?
did you like to walk on water?
were you scared
to be alone

62

I sneaked you in this house, you know. From the hospital. I waited till he went off to work. Then your Aunt Mamie and me, we sneaked you upstairs and into your room. I had your clothes hid in the back of a drawer. A complete layette. Pink. From head to toe. Before you were born I used to go into the room and lock the door. Then I'd take them out secretly and look at them. I'd cry. Well, I'd say, if nobody else wants her around here, then she's mine. My gift of God. Did I tell you that? Yes, Mama, you told me that. I was always a very light sleeper. One night I woke up with this funny feeling. I ran into your room and there he was. Your father. Standing over your crib. Looking down at you. With murder in his eyes. I tell you, if looks could kill, you'd a been dead that night. After that time, I never left you. I saw to it that you never slept alone. Not till you were well out of your crib.

63

just molly and me
and baby makes three
we're happy in
my blue heaven
a turn to the right
a little white light
will lead you to
my blue heaven . . .

Oh, leave that on, Harry. I always liked that song. Mike
used to sing that to me and Dot. But with his own lyrics
that he wrote. After he came around and accepted the
fact that she was there. Listen, Mamie, I don't regret the
hell he put me through. I consider myself fortunate. It
was a jewel in my crown. And I'll spend less time in Purgatory as a result of my trial. But I'll never go through it
again, believe you me. I don't care how much he's crazy
about her now. I remember him when. From before she
became the apple of his eye. The cream in his coffee. The

star tap dancer in the whole universe. Sometimes, you
know, I just sit on the side and I watch the two of them.
She's practicing her routines and he's looking at her like
butter wouldn't melt in his mouth. When I'm really sure
he's in a good mood, I get up my courage. Mike? Mistake!
Mike? Can't you see Dorothy and me are practicing, Flo?
I know, Mike. I just wanted to ask you something. I just
wanted to ask you. Have you ever felt sorry for, you
know, the way you treated me at the time of her birth?
No, Flo, I haven't. I'd be a liar if I said I did. Well, let me
ask you this, Mike. If you had it to do over again, would
you do it any different? He never answers. He doesn't
have to. I know. But it's all right. I'm a God-fearing
woman. And I can forgive. But I can't forget. Harry,
would you turn that up?

. . . you'll see
a smiling face
a fireplace
a cozy room
a little nest
that's nestled
where the roses bloom
just molly and me
and baby makes three
we're so happy in
my blue heaven.

64

How do you feel, Flossie? With your own husband in a
place like that? Terrible, Mamie. But you know why he's
in there? He went down on his knees to the priest and
begged for help. The priest gave him penance and said he
should see a doctor. The doctor gave him pills. And nothing helped. But that's not why he's in there. It's like he
gets possessed by some devil. He hits animals. He howls
when the meat is pink. He rants and raves at the steady
customers. As much goodwill as I build up, he tears
down. But that's not why he's in there. He's in there because of the nightmares. They started again. Where he
thinks he's killing enemy Germans. For one week I had to
wear a towel around my neck. Pretending I had a sore
throat. So the customers that did come in wouldn't see
the bruises. Oh, excuse me a minute, Mamie. Dorothy, I
don't want you repeating any of this to the neighbors or
your Aunt Rose. Rose has the Langan temper. And I don't
want her making any waves when they let Daddy out of
that place. Rose says, give him hell. You know how she

talks. A mouth like a sailor. But I say, let sleeping dogs lay. The crazy thing, Mamie, is that after he hurts me, he hates *me*. If I cry, he says I'm a martyr. Just before he—you know—went away, he said, if I was lookin' to die he'd be glad to accommodate me. I told him God would punish him for saying that. But then when he went down on his knees and confessed it, that he threatened to kill me, the priest said the oddest thing. He said it was his duty to remind him that parishioners who commit suicide are not allowed to be buried in Consecrated Ground.

65

I have to go to the bathroom. Why didn't you say so back at the Ho-spit-al? You said I wasn't allowed in. Do you have to sit down? Yes. Then you'll just have to wait till we get home. It's the car. The bouncing's making it worse. You can hold it. No, I can't. Aunt Mamie'll give you another one of those Wintergreen breath mints. Mamie, give Dorothy another one of those Wintergreen breath mints. I said, no more Life-Savers, Mama. No more what? No more, thank you. Okay. Then read the Burma Shave signs and you'll forget about having to go. There were no signs in the vicinity. That time when I was real little, the shoe was on the other foot. When I locked myself in the upstairs bathroom. Daddy had to climb up a ladder and come in through the window to rescue me. That time, *we* were on the inside together and Mama was locked on the outside. Let me in, Mike. Is she all right? Mike didn't answer. I started to cry. I was sure he couldn't speak because he was so mad at me. He looked so strange I even thought he might hit me, but he didn't usually hit me, only Mama and animals. Then he took two giant steps towards me. He stopped and stared at me. I wondered what I did. Mike, is she all right, for God's sake? The door rattled from her pounding. But there we stood. Completely ignoring her con-nip-tion fit. All of a sudden, he put his arms around me. He hugged me hard. Longer than he ever had before. It made me so nervous I had an accident in my pink cotton pants. But it was a different kind of nervous. It was, you know, happy nervous if such a thing is possible. Mike, answer me, please! Yes, Flo, she's all right. He let go of me. Then, with no effort, he clicked open the lock. The yelling started immediately if not sooner. It's your fault. My fault? Who put the lock down so low on the door? Who put the bastard on the inside? What the hell were you two doing in there all that time? You scared the living daylights out of me! I couldn't get the damned thing open! At that minute, for some reason, I started feeling dirty. It must've been my cotton pants. I hurried away and changed them real quick. Before the fight was over. So Mama wouldn't smell something fishy. Do you still have to go, Dot? Not as much as before, Mama. I guess Mike'll be in that place a long hard time, Floss. I hope not, Harry. No matter how he is, I wish him no harm. That kind of ailment is unpredictable, Floss. Is Mike covered by his Veterans Insurance? You think he could be in a big place like that if he wasn't? It wasn't so bad in there, was it, Harry? Neat and clean, you could eat off the floors. Every night for dinner the patients have to wear a tie if they have one. Mike told Harry the desserts were real good, Flossie. He did? Oh, I'm sure glad, Mamie. A meal ain't a meal for my Mike if he doesn't get his nice dessert.

66

Why is Daddy in that place, Mama? The Veterans Ho-
spit-al? Y is a crooked letter, Dorothy. Y is between X and
Z and that's all you're ever gonna get from me. She bent
down to kiss me goodnight and I asked her to leave on
the light. No! I expected her to say, as usual. It's a waste
of electricity. But she didn't say that. She said, you
weren't mad at me that time, were you, Dot? What time,
Mama? When I didn't take a taxicab home from the Children's Ho-spit-al in Elizabeth? For making you wait outside in the cold for a bus home? After you had your ingrown tonsils out for the second time? I always knew I
should have invested in a taxicab. But it costs an arm and
a leg. And I was so sure the bus would be along any minute. I had no schedule. How was I to know it'd take a
couple hours and complications would set in? You weren't
mad at me that time, were you? No, Mama. Sometimes I
worry where the next dime is coming from. If we'll have
enough coal for the winter. I knew you were still spitting
up blood into your hankie. But you never said anything.

You just sat there on your overnight suitcase. Some day for Christmas I'm going to buy you matched luggage. And I did put you in a doorway to protect you from the wind, remember? Yes, I remember. You don't remember. Kids don't remember anything. Mama, why is Daddy in that place where I'm not allowed? He's—I don't know. He's sick. From the World War. He didn't look sick to me. When I was visiting him today, he told me about this other patient. Who's really crazy. And who really looks it. This patient jumps up and twirls in the air and falls down on his kneecaps. But when you ask him is he a tap dancer, he gets mad as anything. No, dammit, I'm not a tap dancer! I'm a yellow-cab driver! I saw him, Dot. He didn't look like a tap dancer to me. Did he look like a yellow-cab driver? No, Dot, he didn't look like that, either. She kissed me again and went to the door. Just this once, she was gonna leave the light on.

67

What the hell was that racket last night, Flossie? What racket, Mamie? That scrape scraping. Oh, that's Dot's teeth. She grinds them in her sleep. Sometimes all night long. God knows why. I get that when I eat too much candy, Flossie. Did you take her to see a dentist? Sure. I was scared she'd crack a molar, but he said she'd grow out of it. Just like she grew out of the Convulsions and the other stuff. She's always got something chronic. Chronic nosebleeds. Chronic cough. Even when she ain't got a cold. She goes at it till she chokes. I left a light on. Guess it didn't help. Did you hear they electrocuted Bruno Hauptmann? I don't understand a man who climbs a ladder and for no reason grabs an innocent child to leave it lying dead in a shallow grave. There's a reason, Mamie. Money. The root of all evil. I heard they took detectives and dressed them up like priests in the hope that Bruno Hauptmann would confess to the crime. Oh, the church wouldn't allow the confessional used for that. The church would allow anything long as it's in a good cause. And did he crack? Never. Not even to the day they unlocked his cell and marched him down the Last Mile, strapped him in, and turned on the Power. Poor Lindbergh. For a father and a great hero like that to lose his son and heir. Air, Mama? Oh, Dot, you're up. Come have some coffee cake with us. His son and A-I-R, Mama? No, Dorothy, H-E-I-R. His son and heir. Hold out your hand for some coffee cake. Air is the sky. That belongs to God. Heir is the son. That belongs to the man. I held out my hand but I didn't close my eyes. The Cracker Jack taught me a good lesson. My prize had been a top. Very disappointing because I could never make tops work. But Mama still had her prize inside her box and when she told me to close my eyes and hold out my hand I knew she was going to give hers to me. Even so, I was scared to close my eyes. On account of gas masks and stuff. Trust me, Dot, your mother won't hurt you. I felt something drop into my open palm. Wiggling. Jiggling. I opened my eyes. I was holding a big black spider. I dropped it. Mama apologized. She didn't know I'd get so scared. It was only fake. Real, fake, everything scared me. That night, I ransacked the house. Mama never threw anything out and I knew I'd find one of Daddy's old leatherette change purses. I scooped up Mama's spider into Daddy's purse. Being very careful not to touch it. And I put it into my schoolbag. The next day, I went around showing it to every kid I saw. I'd unsnap the purse. And the spider would fall to the ground. Bouncing on her coiled-spring legs. Everybody would laugh their head off. And I'd scoop it up again. With an elaborate flourish. Like it was part of the act. Not like the real reason. That I was terrified to touch it. Carrying it around buried in Daddy's purse gave me a really good feeling, though. Knowing it was there. And not being able to get out. Unless I said so!

Me. I was in charge. In control. I had the Power. So the only person I had to trust was my own self. And I was most certainly never going to be stupid enough to trick my own self. That was a wonderful day. That day of the spider. Scared and thrilled. Showing it to all the kids. I was even popular.

68

You are never to go over my head, do you hear me, Dorothy? Yes, Mama, I hear you. If you want a nickel for candy. And I say no, I can't afford it. You are not to go over my head to your father and ask him. That constitutes stealing. Do you hear me? Yes, but— But, nothing. You have no say in the matter. Charlie Lindbergh must surely have been a great hero. Him having had Christmas decorations made after his own image just like Jesus and all. But Charlie Lindbergh went over God's head. When Charlie Lindbergh stole His sky, he stole God's A-I-R Power. Naturally, God got even. First, being a good planner, God made Lindbergh into a daddy. Then he looked around for an enemy German. God knew that only an enemy German could get as out of line as Charlie. Finally he found Bruno Hauptmann. And that did it. Because, see, when Bruno Hauptmann stole Charlie Lindbergh's son, he stole that man's H-E-I-R Power. As Mama would say, Tit for Tat.

69

Mama and me laughed so hard when Daddy told his funny stories. All about the crazy people he met in the Ho-spit-al. For instance, there was this Veteran who wouldn't trust the nurse to take his temperature. Every time she came near him, he would leap out of his bed, run out onto the balcony, and shove the outside wall ther-mom-eter into his mouth—metal, wood, and all. The nurse would shake her finger at him like she was his mother. He wasn't supposed to do that. Not because the bastard could choke to death. But because the ther-mom-eter wasn't Sterile. Daddy must have told that story a hundred times. And every time he'd laugh till the tears came down his face. At first, Mama laughed. Then she smiled. Finally she said for some reason that story wasn't funny any more. For some reason Daddy stopped talking to both of us. Several days went by. Then one morning he got out of bed and began searching the house. From the attic to the cellar. Mama cornered me in the pantry. Don't tell your father where I hid the gun, Dorothy. I won't, Mama. Flo! Yes, Mike, what do you want? Where the hell did you put my clarinet? Mama smiled. Me, too. Everything was going to be just fine from now on.

70

COMEDY TO BE OFFERED BY
JUNIOR LEAGUE OF ST. CECELIA'S
CHURCH ON ST. PATRICK'S DAY,
MARCH 17.

ISELIN. A gala St. Patrick's
Day celebration is being planned
by the various societies and
groups of St. Cecelia's church
to be held Wednesday night,
March 17. The Junior League
will present the new musical
hit, "As You Were," a play
which abounds in merriment and
lively scenes, elaborated by
catchy musical scores and
pleasing novelties. There will
be twenty speaking parts and
forty-five members of the chorus
will complete the cast.
Miss Veronica O'Zell co-stars

with John Hassey in the major
roles while Charles Monaghan
and Francis Good are equally
important in their lines of comedy. There are very dignified,
but clever juvenile parts, played
by Betty Breen, Genevieve Palac
and Eleanor Burke. Miss Isabelle
Baylis and Eugene Gosselin will
entertain the audience with their
never-ceasing quarrels while
Billy O'Neill as a good samaritan
sends them away happy. Robert
Gosselin, as Jack Trask, is a victim
of a very definite plot to disgrace
him but Francis Johnson as Mr.
Wilbur takes care of the little
matter. Edward Breen will keep the
play in tune with his merry antics
and the chorus of pretty colleens
and Irish jockeys will keep the
play moving smoothly. The novelties
will include Miss Patricia Long, of
Woodbridge, who will offer for the
first time her impersonation of a
French doll, while Miss Dorothy Langan,
also of Woodbridge, will go about the
house dancing and singing "Has Anybody
Here Seen Kelly. . . ."
      —*Woodbridge Independent*

By the time I came out from backstage the auditorium
chairs were all pushed against the wall. Al Ritter and his
orchestra were tuned up. And the social dancing began.
Daddy was a wonderful dancer. Mama actually fell in
love with him on account of him being such a wonderful
dancer. She had come down from the Bronx, New York,

to Woodbridge to visit her small-town New Jersey cousin. They went for a walk in the clay pits. After a couple of hours of wandering in circles the two young girls realized they were lost. They called for help, there was no answer. Suddenly this man climbed out of a pit and appeared on a ridge. Naked to the waist, gleaming with sweat. A spade shovel at his side. Sure he knew the way out he told the cousin. Sure he would lead them back to safety. But only if the little city girl promised to go dancing with him Saturday night. Not if my life depended on it, cried the city girl. Oh please, Floss, begged the country cousin. Oh, all right, she said, anything to get us out of this hole. He made her promise on her honor. She did. Then he laughed. She thought he was making fun of her. But he jerked his thumb over his shoulder. Beyond him, just past the ridge where he stood, was the way out. They were about ten feet from freedom. She could have kicked herself. If they'd gone a few more steps she never would have had to see him again. She'd been tricked by a country bumpkin. That Saturday when the bumpkin arrived at the door in his thick yellow shoes her opinion was confirmed. He would be all over her dainty, graceful feet. She should have worn shin pads. But she'd made a bargain. And she'd stick to it. The first waltz is what did it. He was a perfect dancer. The surprise caught her off-guard. She stumbled over his yellow shoes. The judges saw her. But the bumpkin was so light on his feet he saved the day. His smoothness more than made up for her initial clumsiness. And the judges let it pass. By the end of the evening she'd lost her heart. Lock, stock, and barrel. And together they won the silver cup.

71

the owl and the pussy cat
went to sea
in a beautiful pea-green boat
they took some honey
and plenty of money
wrapped up in a five-pound note
the owl looked up to the stars above
and sang to a small guitar
o lovely pussy
o pussy, my love
what a beautiful pussy you are, you are
what a beautiful pussy you are
pussy said to the owl
you elegant fowl
how charmingly sweet you sing
oh let us be married
too long we have tarried
but what shall we do for a ring?

they sailed away for a year and a day
to the land where the bong-tree grows
and there in a wood a piggy-wig stood
with a ring at the end
of his nose, his nose
with a ring at the end of his nose
dear pig, are you willing
to sell for one shilling your ring?
said the piggy, i will
so they took it away and were married next day
by the turkey who lives on the hill
they dined on mince and slices of quince
which they ate with a runcible spoon
and hand in hand on the edge of the sand
they danced by the light of the moon. . . .

72

Diamonds floated across our faces. And over our bodies. The mirrored ball revolved. The room was a fairy-tale forest. Green balloons. Green flags. Green carnations. The aroma of the Old Spice. The dazzle of the birthday polka-dot tie. The beauty of the blue serge suit. The soft, sweet strains of the waltz. He wasn't wearing yellow shoes. But even if he was I wouldn't stumble. And fall over them like the fat balloons. Dropping from the ceiling. Popping all around us. Making me jump. I looked up at him. He laughed. I laughed, too. Because I knew then that it was all right. He was no country bumpkin. I wouldn't mind being lost with him in the clay pits. Because he'd get me out safely. I could depend on him. Because he was okay now. He'd never have to go back again. To that Ho-spit-al where I was locked out. Away from my own father. Because kids weren't allowed. Any day now, we were gonna pack up and sail away for a year and a day. To the land where the palm tree grows. Do they really grow in Hollywood, California, Daddy? Palm trees? They sure do, pal.

Will you and me and Uncle Nick get to go out there pretty soon? Well, maybe not your Uncle Nick any more. The Deformity isn't Getting Worse. The Deformity is just plain Worse. The Langan Trio will never get together again. But *we'll* get to go out there, you and me, Daddy. Well, *you* might get there, pal. Balloons were popping everywhere. How come just me, Daddy, and not you? Because—because *I say so!* I looked up at him. Because I say so! Do you hear me? He wasn't saying it to me. He was saying it to the ballroom. Over and over. Because I say so! Loud. Mad. People were turning around. I felt my face get red. Because I say so! I didn't know what to do. Then it happened. In the nick of time, Thank God. Al Ritter and his Orchestra went from "When Irish Eyes Are Smiling" into the strains of "Goodnight, Sweetheart." The last dance. The music was over.

73

Do you have any soda crackers, missus? Well, sure, we have Nabisco saltine soda crackers, two to a package. We serve them gratis with our homemade vegetable soup. The negro lady looked at her companion. May we buy a whole box? A whole box? Well, I'd have to charge you retail. I'd lose my profit for the day if I sold you wholesale. That's all right, missus. You mean you want them? Retail? Perhaps. Do you have any unsalted? Unsalted? Our pastor, see, he likes to serve something *neu*tral. Mama looked at the companion. For communion. For communion? You serve Nabisco soda crackers for communion? Mama had Second Thoughts. But it'd been a slow day. So she made an exception. The two ladies left with their saltine soda crackers, retail. Mama went smiling into the rear of the store. Aren't we lucky, Mike. To be born into the Only True religion? Oh, were you taking a nap, Mike? Nothing, I was just saying, here we are. Chosen to be born. Children of God. Don't, Mike. With the Pope, being infallible. And with proper Communion wafers. Mike, don't be so silly. Stop that! Dorothy's out front. She might see.

74

If there was one thing I absolutely loved, it was our second-hand restaurant plates. Because of separations. Separations don't allow runny, disgusting vegetables to Touch. I stared at the empty mashed potato section. I always finished my mashed potatoes first. I saw my face. I moved. I didn't see my face. I looked again. I was back. Gone, back, gone, back. I could actually make my own self appear. With no help from anybody. Chosen by me, myself. To be born. In the potato section. Of a second-hand restaurant plate. Just left of the letter O. O standing for Plaza Lunch. The reason it didn't stand for Plaza Lunch is because we'd already named our place before we found the plates. And Mama'd paid out good money to have gold-gilt letters to that effect painted on the plate-glass window. That marked our place. So she reasoned the letter O was close enough to P. If you squinted. I squinted. The green ribbon bow decorating the edge seemed to become untied. The pointy end moved over to the letter O. And it stuck itself into the circle. Together they made a perfect letter P. With a long tail going around the separations. Separations! The ribbon and the O were Touching! I hit the plate and hurt my hand. I must have said ouch because the pussycat meowed. I got up from the stool and poured some Carnation Evaporated Milk. That pussycat lapped it up. She was almost as beautiful as the Virgin Mary. Gray-striped. With amber-specked eyes. My first pet. So brand new I hadn't even given her a name. I stroked her fur. She was affectionate. Tame. Not like those vicious Protestant dogs. I could feel her bones beneath the fur. So skinny and fragile. I circled her waist with my hands and I squeezed. Not too hard. Wrapped up in a five-pound note. What kind of note weighed five pounds? A music note? A note to the Sister? Oh, forget it, I was just being silly. But certainly this kitten didn't weigh any five pounds soaking wet. This kitten was light enough to swing high. Over my head. Into the air. Oh, lovely pussy, oh, pussy my love. Her marble eyes went wild. She struggled crazily against my palms. Well, sir, if there's one thing I absolutely understand. And do not scoff at. It's fear. I let her down easy. And returned her to her orange crate. She looked as big as a minute. How could anything so small be alive? Already complete with one small head and heart. One set of lungs. One liver. One pair of kidneys. One tail. Two ears. And loins. Did she have loins? She? It was a she. Chosen by God. To be born to grow up and be a mother. To have kittens of her own. It was all set for her. No effort. No problems. No choice. Choice cuts. Four lean loin chops. For some reason, I thought of the meat section of the plate. With the ribbon touching the letter O. And I began to have the Blues. So I consoled the kitten. I petted her faster. Her affectionate purring got funny. Low and kind of moaning. She rubbed against me, like she was flirting or something. For some reason, it made me feel uncomfortable. I suddenly wanted to hit her. With the same hand I just used to pet her. I clenched my fist. Her disgusting contortions reminded me of something. But I couldn't remember what it was. I hated her. How was that possible? To hate something you love? Who could answer that one for me? It wasn't in the Holy Catechism. It wasn't on the list of the Ten Commandments. It wasn't even brought up ever by the nuns when they were giving us good examples for sin-telling in the Confessional. Then what was it? Oh, God-in-Your-Infinite-Knowledge, tell me the answer. Give me something. A word. A sign. A hint. Hint. There it was. H-I-N-T. Stands for Hate Is Not—. T. I couldn't think of anything starting with T. Oh God, make that kitten stop or I'm going to have to bite the sheets to keep my black temper under control. I got up and ran to the rear of the store. I pushed open the door.

75

The room was unpainted. Like an attic. Without beams.
Small. With only enough space for a daybed. To be used
for naps. On slow days. And nothing else. The bile green
army blanket was all rumpled. Showing the great gray
mattress ticking. The lumpy old rose-patterned pillow
had no case. It was thrown aside. Against the window.
With no curtains to hide the small crack in the corner.
Newspapers were scattered all over the bare floor. There
was a smell. Bottom-part-of-the-body smell. Lots of times
of course I'd seen hello smacks or good-bye pecks. Once
in a great while I saw hugs. But never had I seen an em-
brace. With lips actually Touching. I stood so still they
never knew I was there. But the smell was making me
nauseous. And I started to taste something funny.
Starchy. Wonder bread. Potatoes. With salt. Dorothy,
Dorothy, do be good. An obedient child behaves. I swallowed till I got the Saltine taste down. Then I bent over.
Real quiet. And picked up a piece of the newspaper. The
funnies. I closed the door. Making no waves. Bury your

frown down under the ground. Didn't I turn out nice, pussycat? She was sleeping in her box. Next to her Carnation Evaporated Milk. A fly played over the bowl. I folded the paper and swatted at it. In the air. While it was flying. I missed. And hit the plate. It crashed. In a heap at my feet. Then I went outside and sat down and read the funnies. Terry and The Pirates were in big T. For Trouble.

76

No one ever knew exactly how it happened. Everyone must have thought the Proper Precautions were taken. Or maybe each one thought the other took the Precautions. And one of them was careless. Maybe the gateman didn't put on his safety. And the driver got no Stop-Look-Listen sign. Maybe Precautions were taken. But the engineer was going too fast to notice the warning signal. Whatever it was. The big Shell Oil double-trailer plowed smack into the Railroad Crossing. Just drove himself right through. At exactly the same time the loaded freight came bar-relling down the South-bound track. And Pow! Our store, the Plaza Lunch, was only a couple blocks away. So we really felt the explosion. Windows were smashed. Glasses broke. The bed in the back room buckled. And the Moxie Soft Drink mirror fell off the wall. The gateman was a dis-tant Cousin of Mama's. Not blood relations. But they asked her to View the Remains, anyway. And as the *Woodbridge Independent* reported the next day, Positive Identification of Victims, Impossible, Says Fire-Chief.

They had to go through the motions, though. So the doctor lifted the blanket. And Mama stepped forward to View. The Remains of what was supposed to be the third cousin must have got to her. Because right there, on the corner of Green and Maple, in front of the doctor and the Fire-Chief, Mama passed out cold.

77

Daddy was pounding plywood. Boarding up the front windows. The expensive gold-gilt letters were gone. Beyond repair. Maybe the name would be changed now. To match the plates. I was trying to think of a word with O when the doctor came in with Mama. Daddy helped him carry her to the rear of the store. He laid her down on the broken bed and backed out. Respectful. So the doctor could examine Mama's body. He decided to postpone the heavy hammering and busied himself with the broken glasses. Cursing the wanton-waste. Hating the ones that seemed to look okay. But when you viewed them close, god-damn! Another one with a slight chip on the edge! Rendered useless! Invisible Damage! Don't you know, pal, that glasses are expensive! I did know. But I didn't understand what it had to do with me. Naturally, I didn't say that. The devil being in him at that time. And him being, you know, liable to turn on you as quick as he'd look at you. I figured I'd better steer clear. So I inspected the kitten's box. Very important. Looking for cracks in the

Carnation Milk bowl. Leaning close. To detect Invisible
Damage. A thread was hanging from Mama's old maroon
sweater that I was wearing. The kitten pawed at it and
her claws caught. We were stuck. Together. I tried to
break the thread. Carefully. So as not to unravel the
whole darned sweater. Once I saw this Laurel and Hardy
movie. Where Fat had a string on his tie. And Skinny
wanted to be helpful like he usually was. So he pulled.
And pulled. And pulled. And Fat just stood there. Burning. While Skinny unravelled Fat's entire outfit. Tie, suit,
vest, shirt, underpants, and argyle socks went till the
whole thing lay in a heap at Fat's feet. Another fine mess.
God-damn, shit! Another glass wasted! I jumped. So did
the kitten. She ran to the far corner of the orange crate,
dragging the thread behind. And with me after her. Son-
of-a-bitchin' bastard! More Invisible Damage, I thought. I
got so nervous I must have pulled the thread too hard.
The kitten turned. She spit and scratched my hand. I was
bleeding! I hit her. For the first time. And for the last. Oh
God, I hurt her. But she hurt me. I would tell it in confession. Bless me, Father, for I have sinned. How is she,
Doc? Well, she's bound to be affected. What with a double load. But I gave her something to make her sleep.
She'll be okay in a few hours. Thank God. Could you use
a cup of coffee, Doc? Sure could, Mike. I also gave her
something for the other. The other what, Doc? Dorothy,
pass the cream and sugar to the Doctor. Thank you, no, I
take it black. Black? Oh, I could never take black, Doc.
Black's bitter. Why was black always bitter? I looked at
my kitten's black nose. Don't be mad at me, I didn't mean
to make you cry. Mammy's little coal black nose. I
laughed at my stupid joke. Cut it out, pal. Can't you see
the Doctor and me are having a serious talk? I mean, it's
just not like her to pass out cold on the sidewalk. In front
of the Fire Chief himself. It was a tragedy, sure. But he

wasn't even a real cousin. He was several times removed.
Yes, Mike, but it's to be expected, under the circumstances. Yeah, sure. It must've been a terrible sight, God
help us. Terrible. I couldn't leave the store, you know. On
account of the broken glasses. But so what if the glasses
cost me. Just so long as there's nothing the matter with
her. Right, Doc? Right, Mike, nothing the Good Lord
didn't intend. Right. You're a lucky man, you know.
You're going to do land-office business here. The next few
days Railroad execs are going to be buzzing around like
flies. Shell Oil Big-Shots, too. All wanting to be fed. Hey,
I didn't think of it that way, Doc. Out of every tragedy
comes a little ray of sunshine, Mike. Well, I better get
over there. Back to the Scene. I got my work cut out for
me, too. Y'sure have. No, Doc, the java's on the house.
Thanks, Mike. See you around. See you around, Doc. And
congratulations to you and the little missus. Congratulations? She didn't tell you? Oh, I guess she wanted to
surprise you, Mike. Your wife is pregnant. Well, Dorothy.
What'll it be this time? A boy? Or another good little girl
like you?

78

The kitten's not in her crate, Mama. It's down in the cellar. The cellar? Don't go down there, Dot. Why not? Don't ask questions, I'm closing the store. What's the kitten doing in the cellar? Get your sweater! Mama? Daddy threw it down the stairs. Just picked it up and flung it. I always thought cats landed okay, I don't want to talk about it. Is it dead? I'm not taking any more from him! Is it dead? Let's go. Do I have everything? Where are we going, Mama? He has a gun. Is the kitten dead? Its legs are broken. I can save her. She pushed me out the door. Didn't even bother to lock it. She ran off. Down Rahway Avenue, pulling me after her. She kept looking back. Over her shoulder. I can save her, Mama. Oh, my God, Dorothy! What's the matter, Mama? He's coming after us! Look! I looked back. There he was. About four blocks behind us. Is it him, Dot? He's got a gun. My God, what if he shoots us in the back? Look, Dot! Is it your father? I think so. It looks like him. But I'm not sure. Is he running

after us? I don't know. Is he hurrying? Yes, Mama, he's
hurrying. Faster, Dorothy, faster! Now, look, is he going
faster, too? I'm afraid to turn around. He's got a gun! I
think he's going faster, Mama. I can't tell. You look. Yes,
yes, he is. He's going faster, too. Oh God, he's going to kill
us. What'll we do? Jesus, Dorothy, what'll we do? He's
gone. What? He just turned down Maple. He just turned
down Maple? Sure enough. He did. Isn't that something?
I feel embarrassed. But, I mean, couldn't you swear he
was after us, Dot? Didn't it look that way to you? Wasn't
I just-ified? I mean when we went faster, didn't he seem
to go faster? And you know he has a gun. Hi, Dot. I
looked around. There was no one. Up here, Dot, in the
window. I looked up. Who's that, Dorothy? She's a kid in
my class. Where you going, Dot? I looked at Mama. She
kept the bruised side of her face turned away. Oh, we're
going to New York. For a nice vacation with Dorothy's
grandma and grandpa. Ain't we, Dorothy? Say hello to
your little friend. Hello. She was so completely pretty, I
couldn't believe it. She was all smiles and dotted Swiss
curtains. She looked so—I don't know—safe. In a room all
to herself. She probably had matched luggage. She wasn't
interested in stuff like kids being scared. Running in the
streets. Down Rahway Avenue. So they wouldn't be shot
in the back. By guns of their own fathers. But I could still
save that kitten. If Mama would let me. Mama? When we
get to Grandpa's we'll have a swell time, Dot. Don't cry,
Mama. There'll be no more yelling and no more fighting.
It'll be a real vacation, you'll see. Oh, God. Oh, God. People are looking, Mama. We'll go to Radio City Music Hall
and see the great stage pageant. And we'll take the ferry
to the Statue of Liberty. That's a terrific attraction. Can I
ask you something, Mama? And we'll have mashed pota-

toes and chicken cro-quettes at Horn and Hardart's Cafe-
teria. We'll do it up good. Money is no object. Mama? No,
I am not crying! That's not what I wanted to ask you,
Mama.

79

I stroked the green mohair. The train seat was stamped.
With an old repeated pattern. It was rough. No knots
anywhere. My fingers felt something. Invisible damage? I
pulled. Nothing unravelled. It just came right out. A hair.
Stiff. I never hated a stiff hair. Not like I hated a kinky
hair. But this time, I had this crazy wanting. To throw it
on the floor and stamp on it. To hurt it, beat it, kill it! I
crushed it between my fingers and it broke. Like a bone.
Fragile. Skinny. Sweet. Gray. Oh, God, I'm sorry. I would
never hurt it. Not on purpose. But I did hurt it. Didn't I?
When she scratched me, I actually hit her. And I also said
I hated it. So it's possible I made a wish. That she'd die.
And then I forgot it. Evil Intentions. I mean, you have to
be On Guard every minute of the day. Or those Impure
Thoughts, they get out! They get out! And then nothing
can save the one who's Cursed. All the king's horses and
all the king's men can't save it. Let alone me. How could I
save anything? What was it you wanted to ask me, Dot?
Nothing, Mama.

80

We entered her somewhere below the skirt. We inched along the curve of her calf. Past the kneecap. Through the widening of her thigh and into her lower region. Then her belly swelled around us. Her waist indented like a paragraph. It pressed us closer together. Her belt crushed us. Our voices echoed against the metal. And bounced back into our faces. What, Mama? I can't hear you. I said, I can't make it. She bent over the fountain and sucked up a drink. I'm bushed. She sank her body onto a bench. You go on without me. I don't want to go on without you. Yes, Dorothy, I'll be okay. You get up there to the top. I don't need to get up there to the top, Mama. Listen, Lady Jane, I paid two full admission prices and by God, one of us is gonna have the experience of the whole trip. I've had enough experience, Mama. Honest. You haven't had enough experience. You just go ahead. Don't worry about me. I wasn't worried about her. I was worried about me. I hated it in there. A lot. And all I wanted in the world was to get back down with her to the earth. Where everything is safe and sound. She shoved me. And I fell forward into the line. There they were. All her tired and poor. Laughing and joking. All her huddled masses. Carrying souvenirs and sucking Fudgicles and eating frozen Milky Ways. And there was me. Her wretched refuse. Yearning to breathe free. Homeless and tempest-tos't somewhere in the vicinity of her left hand. We shuffled out of the book she carried, up into the rib cage. Her, you know, breasts were hidden in the pleats of her blouse. But I knew. They were there. I looked away from that Impure Thought. Towards heaven. Sweet Jesus, it's high. So much farther to go. Oh God-in-Your-Infinite-Wisdom, I truly believe that this is one Trial and Trib-ulation you inflicted on me that I am not going to pass. But as we approached the narrowing place of her throat a real strange thing started to happen. Oh, I was absolutely terrified like always. But I also began to feel something I'd never felt before. Brave. Sure, my scalp tingled. Yes, my cheeks were hot. Of course, my heart pounded. But none of it mattered. I didn't seem to care that there was no turning back. I just let myself go. I allowed my body to be pulled. Out of the throat. Flung. Across the tongue. Sucked. Up into the sinuses. Pushed. Past the brain. Pressed. Towards the fur-rowed brow. But it wasn't until I was dumped onto the platform behind the eyes that I let myself stop and recognize the terrible truth. I was inside the head.

81

These two eyes are just too big. These two eyes see entirely too much for their own good. These two eyes are making me dizzy. Trying to make me take in the entire Universe. In one fell swoop. Sea. Sky. Space. Heaven. Angels. God. Satan. Devils. Hell. Eternity. Limbo. Purgatory. H-e-l-p! I'm gonna pass out cold before the entire congregation. Here I go. Ready, set, wait a minute! It isn't me that's dizzy. It's the head. The head is *swaying*. Mother of Mercy, what if the head falls off? And we're all dumped out! Into the air! I'm going to throw up. I gotta get out. Excuse me. May I? I gotta get in the line! Please! I know it's not my turn. But I'm in an awful hurry. My mother is waiting for me down in the stomach. And if I don't get back to her right away, she's liable to get scared and throw up. Thank you. Why are you all going so slow? Acting so devil-may-care? Hey, everybody in this place, can't you understand what's happening? Hey you, kid, smugly eating the Snickers bar, don't you know you're in danger! Don't you feel it? The sway? Doesn't anybody else feel it? Nobody but me? Hey everybody, I'd like to make an ann-ouncement! Could I have a little quiet and stop waving souvenir pennants? I'd like to inform you that we are trapped inside of this statue! And this statue is trapped inside of the air! And the air is trapped inside of the sky! And the sky is trapped inside of the Universe and the Universe is trapped inside of God's head! And at any moment, ladies and gentlemen, this Terrific Attraction could come falling down. Killing every one of us in one fell swoop. Because we happen to be too small to leave without our Mothers and too big to have Convulsions. Oh, God. Oh, God, let me out! Oh, how was it, Dot? Up there at the top? It was swell, Mama. Didn't I say you'd love it? It's one of those experiences, isn't it? Yes, Mama. The kind you never forget. Yes, Mama. And certainly never regret. No, Mama.

82

Grandpa, can I listen to your Railroad Watch? Of course, little girl. Tick. Tick. The grapes are ripe. Time for tasting. They're not washed, Grandpa. Oh, you have to eat a peck of dirt before you die. A bee buzzed around the cluster. But I didn't jump at the sound. It was nothing compared to fighting and yelling. Mama says we'll never have to go back there. Back to Woodbridge. Mama says we're gonna stay here with you and Grandma until the day we die. How many ticks before I die, Grandpa? Thousands, maybe. Millions. And then Jesus will come and get me? Yes. In a golden chariot? Well, now, I don't know, little girl. Jesus is very smart. He knows how impressed we all are with golden chariots and stuff of that order. Who wouldn't jump at the opportunity to go off in high style? And since like goes to like, heaven would soon be crammed with lovers of luxury and lukewarm rich Catholics and no working people to do the labors of the spirit. So what happens is this. With parchment proclamations, trumpets blasting, and drums pounding, The

Prince rides into town. Down the Main drag. In a multicolored coach. With wheels of white and spokes carved of gold. With up-holstered walls. And plump pillow seats under satin breeches. And a velvet cape. With a clasp of silver reflecting the crown. And a scepter specially designed to make you go blind from the sparkle if you've not already gone deaf from the fanfare. Meanwhile, far from fortune's false tune, something else is going on. At the other end of town. In the opposite direction. Far from all the pomp and hullabaloo. Out near the dump. Where the smells are rancid. And the road is rough and rarely travelled. Way out there. Via the remotest route. Unheralded. Unannounced. Unseen. Sweet *de*vious Jesus comes ridin' in. In the center of a pumpkin seed.

83

Mickey's here, Floss. Mike? Here? I won't see him, Ma.
He's your husband, my girl. It's your Catholic obligation.
Is it my Catholic obligation to be beat up again? To be
told this baby ain't his either? Just like with Dorothy?
Shhsh, shhsh. She'll hear you. Oh, kids don't understand
such things. That's why they're lucky. She ain't mine,
Flo. That's what he said. Remember, Ma? And now look
at her. She's the spittin' image of him! Did you ever give
him reason? No, Ma, never. Well, jealousy is an unreason-
able demon. Respect his pain. Does he respect mine? You
don't know what I've been through, Ma. You're married
to a Veritable Saint. A Veritable Saint? Does a Veritable
Saint drink wine from hard-grown grapes that could be
used for jams and jellies and the like? Is that your idea of
a Veritable Saint? Well, I'm not going in there and face
Mike. You are going in there and face Mickey and that's
final. He's your man and he's waitin' in the parlor in a
blue suit and tie. Will you and Pop go in with me? No.
What if he hits me? Oh, all right. Yes, we'll go in with

you. Thanks, Ma. Okay, Dorothy, you wait here in the hall and play with the Bevelled-edge mirror like you like to do. Are we going to have to go back, Mama? No, Dorothy. Promise? Where did I say we'd go next? To Barnum and Bailey's. Yes, Barnum and Bailey's. With the clowns and freaks and wild animals. I'm taking you there tomorrow, I promise. Okay, Ma. I'm goin' in there now and face Mike. Mama? Yes, Dot, what is it? I'm in a hurry! Can those wild animals ever get loose? No, Dot, they can't. They're all locked up. Behind bars. Safe in their cage.

84

The image was absolutely normal. Until I moved to the Bevelled edge. Then the left eye sloped down. The nose-hole flared. Pulling my upper lip into a snarl. The bottom lip drooled. Bubbles of spit. I spit again. The bubbles ran down my chin and became em-bedded in the center of a cut-glass star. Behind the hall mirror. On the other side of my re-flection. Inside my Grandparents' parlor, I heard my father sob. Don't cry, Mike, please, don't cry. Then come back, Flo. I can't stand it. I'da put a bullet in my head if I wasn't afraid I'd lose my ever-lasting soul. Silver prisms. Colored rain-bows. Crystal wings of light. Pan, Pan, Peter Pan flew to Never-Never Land.

85

We were home in less than a week. When it started. All
that pleading and begging. All that sobbing and stuff.
Down on his knees. All those promises. Broken. Hers. Not
his. He never promised to take me to see the freaks in
Barnum and Bailey's. He never promised me chicken cro-
quettes and a terrific experience inside of Liberty's head.
He never said I could stay and listen to Grandpa Shannon's watch till the day I died. At which time. Tick, tick.
Jesus would come. Via the Remotest Route. To ride me
out of the Bronx. To join Eileen Langan, aged three, and
all the rest of the children who died, causes unknown. He
never promised we wouldn't have go back there. But
what else can I do, Dot? I'm not able to earn a living.
And your Grandpa can't afford to support us till I'm back
on my feet. Not to mention till the baby is grown. Don't
have the baby. Oh Dot, babies are like ingrown tonsils.
They must come out. Say good-bye to Grandma. And
Grandpa. But you said. I know what I said. But this time,
he did something he never done before. So say good-bye

and let's go. What did he do? He got down on his knees
before me. Right in front of God and your Grandparents.
And he swore he'd never again subject me to that inhu-
man kind of treatment. But you said! It's just like after
the War, Ma. He got over it then. Do you recall? All I recall is, I never wanted you to marry him in the first place.
Well, where the hell else can we go? How about to Aunt
Rose's? Or Aunt Mamie's? Or Aunt Ann and Uncle
Nick's? Aunt Ann and Uncle Nick are as hard up as
we are, Dorothy. But they don't fight. There'll be no
more fights. I promise you. Okay, kiss your Grandma
and Grandpa good-bye. Good-bye, Grandma. Good-bye,
Grandpa. Grandpa? Could I listen to your watch one last
time? Certainly, little girl. Tick, tick. Her promise didn't
mean anything. I finally understood that. And the way it
turned out, it was actually okay. That way, I wasn't disappointed when all of it started again. That way, I wasn't
surprised when it got worse. Worse than before. When we
could still run away. Down Rahway Avenue. Past the little girl with the dotted Swiss curtains. But now she was
Close to her Time. Tick, tick. So she had to stick it out.
Now all she could do was pray to Merciful God in
Heaven for the strength to put up with the fighting. And
the hitting. And the screaming. All but the Whispered
Accusations. They are what hurt her too much. She tried
to steer clear of him. She'd wait for hours. Tick, tick. Till
she thought he was out. But he was somehow always lay-
ing in wait for her. On the stairs up to the bathroom. In
the narrow doorway into the kitchen. His eyes daring her
to pass. And when her weak bladder or her Increased Ap-
petite made it impossible for her to wait any longer, tick,
tick, she'd pull in her stomach with not much success and
she'd try to squeeze her way through. And that's when
he'd let her have them. The Whispered Accusations.

Under his breath. You know. In that terrible quiet way.
Like that man in the straw hat with the satchel did to me
that time. Tick, tick. In the subway. On the way to Coney
Island. Hi, there, little bitch. How's your pussy, little
bitch? Leave me alone or I'll call a policeman. Foul,
whore, go fuck yourself with an unripe banana! Let me
by, Mike. Or so help me, this time. Tick, tick. I'll have
you put away! Oh, my God! No, Mike! Don't! I didn't
mean it! I won't have you put away! I promise! Put those
down! That's our dinner! Those cost good money, Mike!
One-potato hit her in the mid-section. Two-potato got her
on the back of the calf as she ran. Three-potato caught
her on the temple as she ducked into the pantry. Those
potatoes are hard as rocks, Daddy. It's none of your business, Dorothy! But—! Do you want some of the same? No!
Then don't ask for it! Yes! I *want* some of the same! The
butter dish knocked my glasses clear across the table.
They didn't break but the grease blurred my eyes for the
whole rest of the night. Tick, tick. And the next day, the
Sister yelled at me for not having my Catechism assign-
ment done. I took the half-finished paper from her and
went back to my seat to try to complete it. An essay enti-
tled, The Gift of the Magi. The sun started to stream in
through the glass. And the kids started to complain about
a funny smell. Something like cat pee or a dead mouse.
The Sister granted permission for a search of the desks
and the cloak closet. I searched right along with them.
But I knew they wouldn't find anything. The day-old
margarine he threw at me had turned sour overnight. And
when I got up, he wouldn't let me use the bathroom facilities. So I pulled a scarf over my dirty hair. And I went to
school. Where I pretended to look for a dead mouse or a
stray cat. Just like all the other kids with clean hair. So
they wouldn't realize the smell was coming from me. A
couple of kids started glancing over in my direction.

Maybe they were getting wise as to who the culprit was. Oh, God, if you will let me make it home I'll heat a pan of water and scrub my hair till it shines. Please, God. I kept watching the clock. Tick, tick. Why doesn't it ring? Tick, tick. At last, the bell went off. Tick, tick. And I ran out into the free, fresh air. I was safe. I'd gotten out just in the nick of time. Tick, tick. But as I passed two of my classmates, I thought, I just thought, I heard one of them say something that sounded like Meow.

86

And where the hell do you think you're going? I must get out, Mike. It's an absolute necessity. Dorothy takes care of absolute necessities. Send her to the store. She was in her last weeks. And he wasn't in any mood to suffer humiliations. Like letting the entire town witness the disgusting physical evidence of her Mortal Sin. But this most absolute necessity was Holy Mass. She made up her mind she wouldn't knuckle under in that one department. So that morning, she had dressed in secret. Put her rosary into her purse. And sneaked down the stairs. She blessed herself and turned the knob. The door opened. He stood in front of her. Get the hell back to your room. Don't swear, Mike, it's Sunday. I know it's Sunday. Haven't I just been to mass and Holy Communion? Then why won't you let me go too? I'm hungry from fasting. I want my breakfast. It's all ready, Mike. On the kitchen table. I can't eat off the kitchen table. The kitchen's filthy. How am I supposed to clean when you won't let me make a blessed move without your threatening me? The whole damned house is a pigsty. It's not a pigsty, Mike. I got up at five A.M. While you were still sleeping. I went over the whole place with a fine-tooth comb. It's clean as a whistle. Ain't it, Dot? He reached in front of her and closed the door. Then he went out the back way. Mama stood there. Why didn't she do something? Take some money and plenty of honey. And turn the knob and run? Then I could go too. Back to New York. Back to no school. Back to grapes and Grandpa's watch. He came in. Carrying a huge green garbage can. He took off the cover and dumped the contents all over the kitchen floor. Eggshells, orange rinds, coffee grounds, tin cans, potato peels. And near the hall door, an empty Rice Krispies box. On the back was a puzzle. Mama cried out as he pushed her into the kitchen. I should have been scared for her. I should have tried to help her. But for some reason, I just stood there staring at that puzzle. And the prize they were giving away. A ring. Not even a great ring. A plain ring. I wasn't even crazy to have it. But solving that puzzle suddenly became the most important thing to me. I had to win that plain old ring. But Daddy stood in the way. I took my life into my hands. I moved towards the box. Would you agree with me, Flo? That this place is a pigsty? Yes, Mike, it's a pigsty, all right. He stepped back. His heel came down. The box was crushed. The puzzle would never be solved. The ring was lost forever. Forever? Surely, not forever. Are you willing to get down on your knees and clean it up? Yes. Are you willing to forget about putting in an appearance at Holy Mass? I am. And will you send Dot out for any absolute necessities? Yes. And dear pig, are you willing to sell for one shilling your ring? Said the piggy, I will.

87

How about if I stood up to him, Mama? Maybe he'd back down and we could get out. He wouldn't back down to the pope on a bike. What if I answered him back and took my chances of getting hit in the mouth? He wouldn't hit you, Dorothy! I'm the main one to him! If you cross him he'll kill *me!* And if I die, *you'll* be responsible. I was certainly scared of his insane temper, all right. But I almost hated her. Forgive me, God, but she had me hogtied with her Trepidations. If it was just me that would have got whacked I'd have done it. In fact, I think I'd have enjoyed it, if such a thing is possible. At least then, I'd have gotten it off my chest. And I wouldn't have to bite the sheets every night after I said my prayers. But if he killed her because I took the bull by the horns. God-in-Heaven, a child couldn't be responsible for her own mother's death, could she? No. So he went on yelling. And she went on screaming. And I sat quiet. Swallowing Green Bile and drawing pictures of glamorous ladies. Mae West. Lady Guinevere. Hawaiian Princesses. All in long skirts.

It wasn't that I didn't like short skirts. It was that I couldn't figure out how to draw legs. So my ladies just stood there. Stock still. Pretending like they weren't aware that they never walked. And acting like they didn't care that they couldn't run.

88

I don't know when it started. But one day I noticed it. I was standing right in front of him. And he was staring straight through me. I dropped a pencil. No reaction. Was he punishing me? Or was he not punishing me? Maybe he really didn't see me. Maybe I wasn't there. Of course, I was there. A kid couldn't just disappear. Even so, I got anxious. I started carrying stuff around. Dumb things, like wadded-up Kleenex. I started touching everything. For luck, I said. But I knew why I was touching everything. I divided my toes into three parts and moved them in a constant rhythm. Long as I kept the movement going I knew I was there. Sometimes, I'd forget. Then he'd pass me with no sign of recognition. And I'd start to panic again. I'd beat my toes like mad. Then he'd move away from me and I'd feel myself fading away. Like the Cheshire Cat. Invisible Damage. I looked around. Terrified. Mama was there. I smiled. She only half-smiled. But at least she saw me. I existed. She went into the other room. I began to fade. I ran after her. I smiled, she frowned.

But I saw that she saw. And long as I could see *her* seeing me, I knew I was there. I realized what I had to do. I had to never leave her sight. I would follow her into the grave.

89

I don't want that child to see this! I won't have it! I don't care what you do to me! Kill me if you want! But don't hit me in front of that child! No more! I was grabbed and shoved into the hall. I was wrapped in a coat. A wool scarf was wound around my neck. And a tam was pulled down over my ears. My left ear bent. I tried to unbend it but she was shoving my hands into my gloves. The angora ones. That she only let me wear for good. Good meant something special. Maybe we were getting out again. Maybe we were going to New York. Oh, thank you God-in-Your-Infinite-Wisdom, thank you God-in-Your-Infinite-Generosity. Mama, is it true? Are we really going back to New York? She answered by shoving me out the door. Well, I've been shoved a lot in my time. This way. That way. But I was never shoved like that. I don't even want to admit this, it's so awful. But it felt like she wanted me out. Like my own mother was *glad* to get rid of me. Was that possible? Of course not. But her hand felt so mad. At what? What had I done? I was starting to ask that question a lot. What did I do, Mama? What did I do wrong? I never did get an answer. The door slammed shut. And locked. She had locked me out. I was alone. Worse than alone. I had been without a father who saw me. Now I was without a mother who saw me. With no parents left to see me, how could I be sure I was there? I had to go somewhere. Where there were people and I could see them seeing me. I had to run. Before it was too late and I was gone. But I couldn't think of any place to go. There wasn't a kid in sight. Maybe to somebody's house. But Mama said, don't tell the neighbors. So that was out. I could fade away entirely before I got to the church. It was too far. So that was out. It was hopeless. No place. No kitten. No one. Wait a minute! There was someone. And that someone knew about Predicaments. At this very moment, that someone was probably on His way by bus or pumpkin seed. To rescue me. I started to get my confidence back. I went down the porch steps. The second one squeaked. I knew He'd find my neighborhood. Via the Remotest Route. Because when no one else loved a person, He loved. And it was just a matter of time. Tick, tick. Before He'd arrive. And take me to Heaven. I was saved. I sat down under the tree to wait for Him. I waited for hours. He never showed up.

90

You can't go. Why can't I, Mama? Because I say so. But I went with you the last time. Not to the Ho-spit-al. They won't let kids in a Ho-spit-al where babies are being born. Am I supposed to stay here with Daddy? No, you're supposed to stay down the street with the Cahills. I made all the arrangements weeks ago. I don't understand. You will. When you're older. Uncle Harry put the suitcase in the car and got in. Aunt Mamie was already in. They were all hurrying. And whispering. Even though they knew he was on the night shift in his new job at California Oil. Night shift or not, she expected him to show up. She wouldn't put anything past him. They were all piled in. They closed the doors. I stood under the tree looking at them. Aunt Mamie reached out the window to hand me something. Happy birthday, Dorothy! A Halloween pumpkin. On a wooden wagon. I looked through one triangle eye. Orange cellophane. And inside that, nothing but licorice black seeds and chicken corn candy. My birthday wasn't for another month. Why was she giving me my present this far ahead? I didn't want it. I wouldn't take it. She could keep it. The motor started. I reached out and took it. They all waved. I didn't wave. I had my hands full with the pumpkin. The car started to pull away. I trotted alongside it. Mama? What, Dot? I'm in a hurry. I just wanted to ask you. While you're in the hospital, could you die? Well, uh—yes, Dorothy, I suppose I could. I stopped running. I put the wagon down on the ground. I turned away from the car and went along the dirt walk to the Cahills'. Pulling that dumb pumpkin behind me on its crooked wooden wheels.

91

Bungalow. What a glamorous thing. To live in a bungalow. With waxed hardwood floors. Neat closets. Cutouts of the Campbell Soup kids pasted on the kitchen chairs. A pregnant cat and a two-party-line telephone. I slept with their only daughter Ruth. Who had a bedroom all to herself but twin beds. She played the piano and owned an ivory dresser set. It was perfect. And it was quiet. I wished I could stay in that bungalow forever. But arrangements like that could never be made. I didn't really belong there. There was no place for me. On a small, highly polished end table in the living room stood four silver-framed pictures. I wanted to be in one of those pictures. Everyone looked so happy. One was of Mr. and Mrs. John J. Cahill smiling in their wedding finery. One was of Mr. Cahill, the granddad, smiling in his Easter suit. One was of Ruth, smiling in her first communion dress. And one was of a little girl I didn't know. She was smiling too. But she was blurred and old-fashioned looking. Like a painting in an old storybook. Who is that, Mrs. Cahill?

That's Ruthie's big sister. I thought Ruth was an only child like me. Pretty soon you won't be an only child anymore. Yes, well, where is Ruth's big sister now? In heaven. She died before Ruthie was born. What was her name, Mrs. Cahill? Her name was Dorothy.

oh, the lady in red
the fellas are crazy
for the lady in red
she's a bit bawdy
but lawdy
what a personality

I was made up with cake rouge and costumed in the
piano shawl. Ruth was my accompanist. When company
came on the weekend, we put on a fine show. The company applauded and Ruth and me were the center of attention. We were allowed to get excited and have ham
and turkey sandwiches. The turkey was a little pink. I
looked around appre-hen-sively. Nobody seemed to notice but me. So I ate two sandwiches. And nobody said I
was a revoltingly rude pig. During the week we did
terrific family stuff. Like playing cards. Go Fish or Old
Maid. And once we all piled into the Cahills' car. They
had a car. And we drove all the way to Perth Amboy to

the Majestic Theatre. We saw Fred Astaire and Ginger Rogers. And I decided I wanted to grow up to be Ginger and dance with Fred and wear a Marabou boa. I tried to picture Fred living somewhere out there in Hollywood. At that very moment. While he was up on the Majestic movie screen. In two places at once. I wondered what Fred was doing out there in Hollywood. Probably playing Go Fish or Old Maid. Probably not. Probably he was out together with Ginger. Dancing cheek to cheek. And finding the happiness they seek. Right there in the movie theater, eating my Nestlé's Crunch, I began to have this Incredible Dream. About Dorothy Cahill. Actually, about Dorothy Cahill's parents. Mr. and Mrs. John J. Cahill were very modest. But they didn't mind hugging and kissing right in front of Ruth. And for some reason it didn't make me feel bad like when I saw my mother and father. Besides the hugging and kissing, Mrs. Cahill was a good housekeeper and a very moderate drinker. And Mr. Cahill never yelled or hit or threw the pregnant cat down the stairs. He wasn't the type who had a gun and when the kittens were born I was sure he wouldn't drown them like some people. He would keep them all. And if he couldn't keep them, I was convinced he would set them loose in some rich Protestant neighborhood where they threw out end cuts of roast beef and buttered carrots. Anyway, this was my dream. Dorothy Cahill was dead. And some night soon, when the Cahills were asleep, I'd sneak my picture into Dorothy's frame. From then on, they'd be sure I was their Dorothy. And it would be years before anybody noticed the difference and sent me home.

93

But you've been here over a week, Dorothy. I'll go tomorrow, Mrs. Cahill, okay? But don't you want to see your own father? Yes, Mrs. Cahill. Then why don't you go ahead, Dorothy. You have to go home some time. Home? I looked over at the picture on the highly polished end table. Mrs. Cahill didn't know it, but we had a secret. Didn't we, Dorothy?

94

I trudged across the burnt grass. The night felt like an oven. The sky was the color of ashes. The house was gobbled up by shadows. The screens had been left on too long. Rusted brown over the shut windows. The shades were down. My mouth got dry. My heart beat like the devil. If I'm lucky, he won't be in there. Please, don't let him be in there. My face got warm. Forgive me, Lord, for saying that about a person's own father. I skipped the squeaky second step. I didn't want to be given away. The screen door had a loose nail. If I'm lucky, I'll cut myself on it and have to hot-foot it back to the Cahills' for a Band-Aid. I tried the handle. Locked. Good. I pressed slightly. It turned. Not locked. Bad. Inside, the hall was still. Daddy? I peered up the stairs. Blackness at the top. I thought I saw something move. Scrape, scrape. Daddy, are you up there? Must have been a tree against the bathroom window. I drew back the dark drapes into the living room. I tripped as I tried to tiptoe past the upright piano. I got this sudden urge to pound on the keys. To sing, no, scream at the top of my lungs. I've heard Hawaiians play in the land of the wicky-wacky, but I must say, you can't beat Turkey in the Straw, by cracky! Something caught my eye. A dim light reflected on a couple of the white keys. Electricity cost good money. It wasn't to be wasted. So any time a light was left on in our house, it could only mean one thing. Somebody was home. I knew that, now. I also knew where it was coming from. I began to feel sick to my stomach. My head felt like it was coming off. I was sweating. I wished I could go swimming or go sit in the bathroom, with my head on the sink till it went away. Please, God, don't let me throw up. I swallowed hard and looked around the living room to get my bearings. The armchair. The matching mohair sofa. The gate-legged table with the drawer for broken stuff. The fireplace with the two matching owl andirons. The big brown radio. Mama's porcelain painted saint. The small bookcase. With one sample copy of the *Encyclopaedia Britannica*, letters Q–R–S; one *Bobbsey Twins Go to Summer Camp;* one *Gold Medal Cookbook;* one Mass Missal; one Sears Roebuck catalog, Fall-Winter; and one copy of *Elmer Gantry* with the bad pages torn out by Daddy after him and Mama read them through. For some reason, I had put on Mrs. Cahills' piano shawl. I wiped my face with it. The fringe tickled my nose and made me more nauseous. I couldn't take any more time. I trotted across the room. Towards the dim light. Coming from the dining room. I stopped at the divider. I looked inside. And I saw my father.

95

The floor was littered with empty sardine cans. Oil stained the linoleum where they'd been dumped. Jagged edges. Bile-Green flies buzzing. The dining room table was covered with a soiled mattress. From the ceiling, one bare bulb. A moth flew crooked around the dim light. Yellow above his head. A fly landed on his face. He didn't move. He sat perched on the mattress. Naked to the waist. His belly-button showed. I'd never seen it before. His underwear was dirty. Hanging half open. I tried not to look, you know, Down There. But I couldn't avoid the smell of his skin. Rancid. Body odor and dead fish. Daddy? He didn't answer. I looked at his feet. They made me feel very sad. Just hanging there with the toes turned in. I wanted to go over and put something under them. A chair. And a pillow. So they could rest. And go to sleep. And fall off and die. My heart skipped. Not heavy. Light. Oh, my God, I was wishing he was dead. How could a Catholic girl think such a terrible thing? His own daughter. But I wasn't his daughter. I was Dorothy Cahill, oldest child of Mr. and Mrs. John J., sister of Ruth. And I had to get home to my family and my bungalow and my two-party telephone. Where everything was spotless and nothing was ever done that you couldn't tell the neighbors. I decided I had to get out of there, immediately if not sooner. But I couldn't move. I was as still as my father. The moth made one last attempt to burn itself up on the faint light. I stared at it. I thought I heard its wings. Beating somewhere in the region of my loins. I felt the heat of my skin. Rising from the bottom part. And I smelled my body's own foul odor of dead fish.

96

Did you see your father, Dorothy? Yes, Mrs. Cahill. I saw him. Was it nice? Yes, it was nice.

97

daddy boarded up
the dining room
and locked us in
we three
four and a half months
we lived in that room
my mama the baby and me
my mama slept on the table
i slept on a cot
the baby was in a basket
i hated it a lot

we'd listen
till he went off to work
then we'd sneak out
for eggs
i'd run around the kitchen
to stretch my stumpy legs
we'd finish our eggs and coffee
then we'd make it neat

so daddy wouldn't go all crazy
'cause we came out to eat

one monday
after christmas day
he let my mama free
the week after that
i came out
the baby
he still wouldn't see
at night we'd go back in there
the reason i forgot
the baby didn't know the diff'rence
i hated it a lot

aunt rose came by
to visit us
bring out the kid
she said
mama says
godinhisgoodnessno
that man would shoot me dead
my mama says
he ain't seen it yet
her face went white as pearl
he don't know if the kid i had
is a boy or a little girl

well
aunt rose brought out
the baby
and laid it in the light of the tree
daddy arrived home
early from the job
and pretended
like he didn't see

so rose picked up
the baby
and shoved it at him
on the spot
i watched him
take my sister
i hated it a lot
. . . . . .

98

During the World's Fair in Paris, France, this man disappeared. This man who disappeared's sister, played by somebody like Merle Oberon, told the hotel owner and his wife. She and her brother had come from the country together to see the Fair. They'd both checked in. And now he was gone. Did they remember the checking in? Yes, they said, they remembered. But she'd been alone. No, she said. She remembered his room number. Next to hers. Number fourteen. They were very patient. Number fourteen? They opened the record book. There was no number fourteen. Would she care to look? She didn't care to look. She knew what she would see. No number fourteen. And only her signature. They continued to be nice to her but the more she insisted they believe her, the more they started to act funny towards her. Like she was a little crazy. Well, what Merle Oberon, or whoever it was, didn't know was this. Her brother had been there just like she said. But that night he had died of Typhoid fever. And the hotel owner didn't want to scare the tourists during the Fair season and spoil his profits. So he had walled up the room, papered over the entrance, and erased the brother's name and number from the record book. Well, Merle began to question herself. Maybe they were right. Maybe her brother hadn't come with her. Maybe she had no brother in the first place. Maybe she was crazy. She began to go into a complete decline. Fainting and carrying on. And she herself might have died the way they did in those days except for an Unexpected Turn of Events. The leading man, I can't remember his name, said he believed her. Immediately, the color came back to her cheeks and she began to rally. After a try or two the mystery was solved. The brother's body was found in an unmarked grave. And Merle Oberon was proved to be as sane as everybody else. But that was a movie. And the people were all actors. Playing out their roles.

99

But how come me? He don't want to lay eyes on the new baby. But how come me? He says he doesn't want us in his sight. So her and me, we have to stay in the dining room. But how come I have to stay in there, too? What did I do? I don't know, Dorothy. So don't pester me. All you have to know is that we're not allowed to come out of that room till he tells us to. Maybe that will be never. Maybe we'll just go in there and never come out again. Just pray, Dorothy, that that won't happen. That's all we can do. Is it because the baby is a girl? Like me? He don't know if the baby is a girl, a boy, or what. And he don't give a damn. He just hammered those two by fours across the room divider. And moved the player piano in front of the planks. You'd never know the room was ever there, would you? But what if after we go in there he boards up the windows, too? He says he's going to. But we'll never see daylight again. After a while, the whole neighborhood and the Cahills will forget we ever existed. Well, they'd send detectives looking. But what if the detectives did come? To investigate Mysterious Goings On? They'd never find us. Behind the upright. Maybe we'll die in there. Maybe. Oh, God, I will do anything in the world to keep from having to go into that dining room. I will beg, pray, lie, scream, and make bargains. I will become a nun. Do missionary work in Mainland China. I will go to Africa to work with lepers. I will make any promise. Only, please God, don't make me go in there. I won't go in there! I won't be an obedient child any more! I don't want to die! Mama carried the baby into the room. I stood outside. She turned and looked at me. I wondered if I could escape some way. I thought of the Toonerville Trolley. Was it still in the drawer? Where I put it that day when I was real little? Even if it was, the wheel had never been fixed. Broken. Beyond repair. There was no escape in it. Where else? I looked around the living room. I saw the glass eyes of the matching owl andirons. I saw the painted saint's porcelain stare. The silent radio. The closed books. Nothing was alive in that room. Nothing saw me. I looked back at my mother. Across the Repeated Flo-ribunda Roses. She smiled. I saw her seeing me. And I followed her in.

100

I guess I entered that room and just went to sleep. Like in a grave or something. The thing is, I don't remember any of it. Plain everyday stuff like, you know, going to the bathroom. How we ate. Where did we wash? I don't know. I must have never told anybody on the outside. About how we were living. Don't tell the neighbors or Aunt Rose. And if I did go out to school I must have kept it from the other kids, from the nuns, certainly from the priest. Bless me, Father, for I have sinned. But I don't know what it is I did. My birthday came this year, but I don't remember it. So that's not my sin. So did Halloween come, and Thanksgiving, and New Year's. I don't remember them. So that's not my sin. Oh, yes, Christmas came, I guess. I don't remember that either, but maybe that was my sin. I mean, Jesus had a birthday, too. But he didn't show up for mine. So why should I show up for his?

101

Funnily enough, there's one little tiny thing I remember. One night I was lying on the cot. With my face to the wall. My mother was sitting next to the radio. Rocking my new baby sister. Singing a lullaby. I turned to look at her. Her blouse was open. And she had the baby sister pushed up against her, you know, bare breast. I thought she was smothering the baby. I wanted to call out. Instead I turned away. Sad and glad. I mean, if I let her do that to the new baby sister, I'd have Mama all to myself. Alone. In that room. And that would be great. Wouldn't it? Sure, it would. Why wouldn't it? After all, my own mother. Out of nowhere, a small black spot appeared on the wall. I didn't have my glasses on. So I couldn't make out what it was. Suddenly, it moved. The spot was coming towards me.

102

In *Terry and the Pirates*, Terry and his best friend were captured and thrown into prison. With no inmates and no lights. For several hours, they just hung around there in the dark. Wondering when they were going to be tortured. Them supposedly having important Secret Information that the Dragon Lady was dead set on getting. The terrible thing was, they didn't know what it was they had. They couldn't have revealed anything if they were given the worst torture. The worst torture could just go on forever. While Terry and his best friend went through Untold Cruelty. Wondering. What was it that the Dragon Lady wanted from them? Wanted so badly she was willing to kill them? After a whole lot of in-stallments, the full moon appeared. At last Terry and his best friend were able to make out a little bit of their surroundings. But beyond that one patch of moonlight coming in through their cell window there was nothing but darkness. Terry began to get this strange feeling. Like they weren't alone. Like something was watching. Getting ready to close in on them. The best friend said it was probably just a trick of the full moon. But Terry, who was always the first to figure things out, peered harder. Past the best friend's shoulder. Into the inky blackness. Don't move a muscle, he warned the friend. He'd discovered what their torture was. They had been locked in the cell with a gigantic spider. Mama! Mama! What is it, Dot? You'll wake up the baby. The baby? Is she still alive? Of course, she's alive. You must have been having a bad dream. A bad dream? I opened my eyes and looked around at the locked room. I turned to the wall. The black spot was gone.

103

Actually, we could have gotten out any time. There was a door. The one that swung open into the kitchen. I was too small to stick up for my rights. But if Mama wanted to, she could have just taken us two kids and walked out of that rotten room. But she didn't. When we first went in there I was furious with her. For letting my father walk all over her that way. I couldn't understand why she took it. There was this fat kid in school who was always such a pest around the bigger kids. He'd keep at them and at them and at them till one of them raised a fist at him. You're gonna get it, fat kid! they'd yell. You're gonna get it, cause you're askin' for it! At that minute the fat kid's eyes would get big as saucers. He'd move closer till his fat face was an inch from the bigger kid's fist. Hit me! he'd scream. G'head, you big bully! Hit me! Hit a kid littler than you! Hit me! And the bigger kid would hit him and he'd stop. But here's the funny part. If the bigger kid decided he wasn't worth the trouble, and he didn't hit him. The fat kid would burst into tears. Like he was disappointed or some crazy thing like that. Why did the fat kid act like that, Mama? Can you tell me why he took it? No, Dorothy, I can't. Kids do weird things. It's not important, but I'm gonna tell you something that is important, Dot. What is it, Mama? Never, *ever*, call a person fat to his face.

104

Aunt Rose came by with a tree. In spite of Mama's tears and fears and protests, she insisted Mama bring us into the living room. Out in plain sight. Well, after a lot of back and forth, Aunt Rose won. Aunt Rose always won. Mama came out first. Carrying the new baby sister. I waited a while. Then when I tried to come out, I started to cry. Mama said it was because I was nervous. And Aunt Rose said it was because I was so relieved. But they were both wrong. That dining room was small. It was dark. It had no air. And it was rotten. But I knew every inch of it. I was at home in it. I didn't want to come out. Why should I? Outside meant big. With shadows and beasts and strangers. And familiar people with guns. I didn't like that world out there. I'd grown to like that small room. I'd gotten used to the smell of no air. I even kind of liked its rotten-ness. When a thing is rotten all the time and you know it's rotten, then you always know what to expect. Oh-my-God, it's him! It's Mike, he's coming! Dammit, Florence! Don't you dare go back in there!

You stay the hell out here where you belong! No brother of mine is gonna bully you any more! He's this kid here's pa, and that's it and that's that! Why the hell didn't you tell us that shit was going on again, Florence? I asked you. Why couldn't you admit it? I was afraid he'd kill me, Rose. He wouldn't kill you. He just threatens a lot. Oh, my God, Rose, here he comes! Sit the hell down, Florence! You, too, in there, Dorothy! You're a member of this family. Get your ass out here! I was standing in a far corner of the room. Behind a chair. Peeking out. He came in. I stopped breathing the no air. I watched while he didn't look at my mother. Aunt Rose picked up the new baby sister and shoved it at him. Congratulations, Pa! It's a girl! It's a little bit late, her being four-and-a-half months old, but better late than never! I expected him surely to have a con-nip-tion fit. But he didn't. I expected him not to take the baby sister. But he did. He stared down at the eyes. Nose. Mouth. Hair. Heir. Air. I could smell it. What? *It!* I started to choke. I swallowed it. My face got hot, my palms started to sweat. But I wasn't mad. I was furious. I wanted to bite sheets. I bit my tongue. I wanted to stamp my feet. I divided my toes into three parts. I wanted to make my eyes roll back into my head and have Convulsions. I stood there. Silent. Swallowing. While he carefully inspected that rotten little face. The rotten little face smiled. Daddy didn't smile. Then he patted the baby's behind two times. Mama made a big sigh. Aunt Rose picked a piece of lint from her sleeve and nodded, importantly. My swallow started to back up into my throat. It's not gonna stay down. Not this time. This time it's gonna fall out on the floor. Wood. Knots. Saw. Plane. And I can't touch it. I clenched my teeth. I clenched my jaw. I clenched my fists. Finger. Nail. Sew. Prick. Pain. Dorothy, are you comin' the hell out here? I clenched my eyes and my divided toes. I crouched further behind the chair. Dorothy! Why don't she come out, Florence? She's staying in there to get attention, Rose. We know you're there, Dot, so stop carrying on. I put my left hand to my mouth and started licking the sweat. Salty. I wasn't crying. I was happy. In my cell. Cellar. Kitten. Stairs. Golden. Shirley Temple. Bojangles. Cocoa Butter. Pretty? Plain. I liked being in my place. I didn't want to come out. In fact, I decided I would never come out again. Not as long as I lived. I am in here forever, I said to myself, as I came out. Smiling and smiling. Out into the air. Plane. Plain. Pain. Plan. Peter Pan. Oh, Dorothy, there you are. Get your ass over here. Like a good little girl. And say hello to your pa. pa. pa . . .

105

. . . .
from then on
we were a family
we even had some fun
the boards
on the dining room door
came down
and daddy put away his gun and
i forgot it happened
like something
i'd been dreaming
till eighteen odd years later
when i suddenly woke up
screaming.